Are you

How to work with NEW **...ensions**

Are you a
Master of Light?

**How to work with NEW energies
from higher dimensions**

Louise Hopkinson and Jane White

Bossiney Books • Launceston

Acknowledgements

This book has been put together with the help of friends, family, therapists and healers, whose wisdom, love and inspiration provided the stepping stones between worlds, and of many other generous people who willingly volunteered their time and skills. Blessings to you all.

From Louise: I would like to thank Andy for his encouragement, patience and tolerance whilst I have been having 'my Spiritual Experience'. Also thanks to Hazell and Christine for their friendship and guidance, and to Peter for his insights and knowledge.

From Jane: An enormous, very special thank you to Paul whose love and support helped bring this project to fruition. Also thanks to Glen and Sheila for illuminating my path.

Illustrations

The inspirational cover artwork and illustrations on pages 161 and 164-5 are by Graham Cheater. Artwork on pages 107, 130, and 162-3 by Alix Wood. Artwork on page 168 by Paul Barlow. Magic eye picture by Matthew Hopkinson. Aura photographs on pages 166-7 were taken by Angela Tarry.

Quotations

Extract from *Signposts* by Denise Linn, published by Rider: used by permission of The Random House Group Limited.

First published 2004 by Bossiney Books Ltd
Langore, Launceston, Cornwall PL15 8LD
www.bossineybooks.com
Reprinted 2006

© 2004 Louise Hopkinson and Jane White

The moral rights of the authors have been asserted.

British Library Cataloguing-in-Publication Data
A catalogue record for this book is available from the British Library

ISBN 978-189938399-3   ISBN 1-899383-99-9

Printed and bound in Great Britain by Short Run Press Limited, Exeter

Contents

Introduction

Louise opened her eyes and quickly turned over in bed to look at her alarm clock. It was seven in the morning and, much to her delight and relief, she was still alive. She pinched herself to make doubly sure.

The reason for her slight uncertainty was that she had just undergone what you might call a near death experience which, although it had taken place while she was asleep, was as vivid in detail as any waking equivalent. Its impact left her in no doubt whatsoever that she still had much to do in her life and that a major project she and I had dithered over for so long should be moved to the front burner.

I first met Louise on one of her spiritual awareness courses. She is a marvellous teacher who has spent much of her working career as head of drama in a local school, but she now passes on to adults the benefit of her great spiritual wisdom and knowledge. Several months after the introductory course finished I joined her Mandala group, a weekly gathering of lovely like-minded people who meet for discussion, meditation, talks and general friendship. It was there she and I began to exchange notes on unusual phenomena we had each been witnessing.

Every Monday evening we would eagerly await the other's news – what had happened since we last spoke? when? where? It seemed that we were being shown, often within similar time frames, spiritual energy as beautiful, vibrant colours we had never come across before in this world. Their luminosity and purity were so distinctive we knew immediately that what we were describing to one another had to be from the same source. Then one night as we were sitting together in Louise's kitchen, we both glimpsed a small blue flame over the wooden table in the centre of the room.

We looked at each other, dumbfounded. There was no doubt at all now about our shared experiences. The question was, where were these colours and images from? We tentatively began to voice what we had speculated in private for some time. Would it be heresy to suggest they were from the fifth dimension?

Late one Monday night Louise's husband Andy, who was sitting quietly after every one else from Mandala had left and was listening to Louise and me chattering endlessly about all these strange goings on, said with some exasperation: 'There's got to be a reason why you two are seeing these things. You're being brought together for a purpose. Perhaps you ought to write a book!' We exchanged glances again and, realising we had been ignoring him, looked rather sheepish. But who on earth were we to take on such a daunting task? There were probably plenty of authors out there already having their books published on this very subject all over the world. However, when we actually investigated, there weren't. We could not find anything which explained to our satisfaction what we were going through. Maybe Andy was right.

We let the matter rest and carried on with our own spiritual practices as though nothing had been said. But frustration at not being able to compare notes through reading about other people's encounters with the colours began to build. Then a spiritually inspired artist, Patrick, gave me a painting of a special friend in the elemental kingdom. In the picture a striking rainbow of unusual glowing shades – principally blue, green and pinky yellow – arcs over his head. I showed this to Louise, who was as intrigued by the image as I was, and not long afterwards she had her memorable lucid dream. Since dreams are often the means by which we receive important guidance, those that imprint themselves indelibly on our minds for days, sometimes months and even years, are not to be ignored. Louise's falls into that category and it is for this reason I now relate it in full here.

As she drifted off to sleep her third eye opened wide and symbols came into view, as though she was about to be given an input of spiritual information. After the symbols came a feeling of being sucked into what she soon recognised was the tunnel traditionally associated with the soul leaving the body. She was aware of people at the end waiting to meet her, but strangely enough they appeared unexpectedly as geometric shapes rather than in human form. She found herself thinking: 'I'm passing over… I was fit and well when I went to bed – I wonder what will happen to my body to bring this about… a heart attack?'

Then, quite importantly given the theme of this book, she determined for herself rather than hearing another's voice that it was not her time to die because there was much more for her to do. This, however, did not halt her journey down the tunnel and she continued to travel onwards. She hastily reassessed her situation and wondered whether fear might be confusing the issue, so she affirmed to herself, 'I have all that I need to fulfil my wants and all that I want to fulfil my needs.' At which point she came out of the tunnel.

The next dream phase took her to a house where she was expecting people to arrive for one of her introductory courses. The door burst open and Sally, in 'real life' a local woman who channels Archangel Michael, strode in with great purpose. Louise was curious as to why Sally, with all her experience and know-how, needed to attend.

Sally interrupted her thoughts by stating that she had been given a telephone number by the ascended realms which enabled people to hear them. And to prove her point she went over to a phone, pressed the relevant digits on the pad and lifted the receiver to allow the sound of celestial singing to fill the room. A couple of course members walked by, talking about third dimensional concerns, and the link was cut.

Sally then explained to Louise that she could also show her which masters were in her aura and working with her. She had various sheets of lighting gel in a wide range of colours, including those Louise and I had been coming across (lighting gel is put over stage lights to create special effects and is designed to take high intensity light and heat). Louise assumed she would need to put her hand under these sheets for one of them to infuse her with its energy, which would signify the ascended beings in her life at that moment – she secretly felt it would be Saint Germain and Djywal Khul. She sifted through the colours in determined fashion and casually remarked that she had come across the 'new' ones before.

As soon as she opened her mouth and uttered these few words, Sally exclaimed, 'That's it! I've been shown who it is.' After the slightest of pauses, during which Louise guessed – wrongly – what was coming, Sally stated emphatically, 'It's Kuthumi!'

Louise confided in me afterwards that in the dream she felt slightly disappointed, and so responded hesitantly. This was interpreted as her not knowing who Kuthumi was, but she quickly reassured Sally to the contrary. And then she woke up.

After pinching her leg, she detached herself from the dream and considered what Kuthumi stands for. He is a highly evolved soul, an ascended master, and is known for his role as a world teacher. As soon as she brought these facts to mind she was filled with the strong belief that the near death experience was a way of confirming for her that she would be embarking on another form of teaching. When she sat up in bed and Andy pulled back the curtains to allow the morning light to enter the bedroom, the sky was filled with a strange rainbow made up of the same colours as those in my painting. She and Andy were now totally convinced this teaching would come about through our collaboration on a book.

A few days afterwards Louise talked me through her astonishing dream that brimmed with potent images, some of whose meanings became even more significant much later. The messages were about taking responsibility, communicating with the ascended realms and working with colour. Her enthusiasm was beginning to infect me. I could not fail to be drawn by the exciting prospect of sharing our experiences with others. We could not be the only ones this was happening to, and it would be fantastic to reach out to those who, like us, had exhausted all currently available information and now felt the urge to push on into uncharted territory.

I wavered briefly. I had already written a short book, and was glad to have gone through that process to learn useful lessons about working with higher vibrations. But I was now faced by a much greater challenge. Did I really wish to make such a commitment? In the end I accepted it with relish, because my inner voice, intuition, call it what you will, was yelling at me it was the right thing for me to do.

Soon afterwards the first of several themes – 'Be a Master of Light' – came to Louise, accompanied by the bizarre sighting of an above average number of bees for the time of year. She also had several intriguing conversations with various people who stressed the importance of bees and commented that, despite their lack of an aerodynamically designed body, they defy the laws of nature (like the two rainbows) and manage to fly. (Rainbows and, to a lesser extent, bees incidentally have continued to play a major part in our work.)

At last Louise and I focused on our intent and sat down together to compile a list of chapter headings. Little did we know that we had just signed ourselves up for a remarkable voyage of learning and discovery that would last several years. It became clear that what we had observed already was just the tip of the iceberg and that the content of our book would be a combination of past and ongoing experiences.

We were continually encouraged to show our own mastery, to live and be what we are now recommending for others. But none of it would have been possible without the continuous support of the ascended realms, friends, family, and workshop volunteers who helped us uncover our unknown. With them we found the proof that we believe will help you gain a clearer understanding of your dear friends the ascended masters, the celestial rays and how to use them in your life, your own and Mother Earth's ascension path, and amazing changes to your energy system. In short, we offer you the chance to reach a deep awareness of yourself as a master of the cosmos.

So here it is: a distillation from our perspective of how and what it means to become enlightened. Read all with an open mind, enjoy experimenting with the practical sections, especially chapters 7 and 8, and listen to your heart for the resonances which will confirm those truths of ours which are also yours. Your divine gifts are there waiting for you to reach out and receive them with God's blessing. May they bring you infinite joy, peace and love.

Postscript
While I wrote this book in the first person, *Are you a Master of Light?* represents an equal contribution of skills and effort. Louise must be given full credit for her vision, commitment, enthusiasm and absolutely brilliant analyses of channelled material. I thank her with all my heart.

CHAPTER 1

The ascended masters – who are they?

For several years after setting out on my spiritual path I would often come across the phrase 'the ascended masters'. Even though I had no idea what or who the masters were, each time I read or heard these words an unexplained thrill of excitement fluttered in my heart. I also felt at some deep level what I can only describe as distant familiarity – like when you're trying to remember a name or a word and it's on the tip of your tongue. You know it, but you just can't bring it to the front of your mind.

Drawn to find out more about the masters, but uncertain as to why or, more to the point, whether they were actually real, one day I was suddenly given unexpected proof of their existence in a very memorable fashion. The event had such a dramatic impact on me that any doubts I had previously were swept away in one gigantic sweep of a spiritual broom.

Louise and I were attending a short workshop whose teacher explained that she 'worked with the ascended masters' and that they would be overseeing the afternoon session. It consisted of a guided meditation during which we were to meet a high level being. As soon as I closed my eyes a deep pink flooded my inner vision, and as the minutes ticked by the pulsating pink was interspersed with violet.

Then an extraordinary feeling of unconditional love flowed through my body, something I had never experienced before with such intensity. The icing on the cake was towards the end of the meditation when in my mind's eye a gift was held out to me in the palm of a hand.

It made tears drop softly down my cheeks, for it was such a personal present, one that only someone who cherished and knew the real me extremely well would ever have considered offering.

The next day the connection was maintained. I was beautifully relaxed – my limbs felt somewhat like cotton wool – but I
was also profoundly tired so I rested whenever I could. Each time
I shut my eyes, streams of fabulous colours cascaded down. I
have since realised that I was being given some welcome healing,
as well as an extra glimpse, just in case I thought I'd imagined the
previous day, of wonderful opportunities to come.

This is not an exceptional incident of course. People all over
the world are beginning to experience for themselves the actual-
ity of the ascended realms. But who exactly are the masters,
where do they 'reside' and what do they do?

The first point to make is that 'master' does not imply any
level of importance, even when it's connected with the even
more potentially emotive word 'ascended'. Take the analogy of a
factory – everyone's job is crucial: from the cleaner to the man-
aging director, each person has a part to play for the smooth running of the whole organisation. Miss out one of the links and
imbalance follows. Although in the universe the masters are,
metaphorically speaking, the more senior partners in the business, they would much prefer us to think of them as our close
colleagues, friends or older brothers and sisters, certainly not elevated beings we should be in awe of or afraid to reach out to for
guidance. Their compassion and love for us are limitless, and
they encourage us every step of the way.

Most ascended masters, unlike most angels, have had incarnations in a physical body, so they fully appreciate what we are
going through. In fact they are constantly in admiration for the
progress we are making even though we ourselves might sometimes feel we are going nowhere fast. A great number of masters
incarnated, often in groups, as innovative thinkers and doers on
earth when there was stagnation of low vibrational energy or
when denser energies were predominating. They helped raise the
light quotient of the world, and brought positive attributes associated with higher spiritual values – honesty, knowledge, wisdom, vision, truth, courage, compassion, acceptance, understanding, and so on – to humanity's attention.

It would be an understatement to say their tasks were might-
ily challenging. As great poets, philosophers, mathematicians,

artists, priests and priestesses, scientists, rulers... these inspirational individuals often put themselves at enormous personal risk to create the crashing waves that would rock political, social and economic boats.

In some cases their ideas, so far ahead of their time, were judged too provocative and threatening. Degraded and humiliated by their contemporaries, they were cut down by people who did not yet understand or appreciate their messages. Commendation came much later from generations who were better able to recognise the enormous leaps forward mankind had taken as a result of their influence. It is no wonder the Bible refers to these enlightened men and women as the great and illumined ones.

Perfection in oneness

While many ascended masters made remarkable contributions during so-called dark ages, it should also be remembered that they and others like them had incarnations as what we might consider ordinary, conventional individuals about whom we know nothing.

They might not have set off flashy fireworks, but they did blaze trails nonetheless. They established a pattern for all to follow: by living modestly according to divine laws, they enriched those with whom they came into contact, and learned and grew spiritually in a steady, unassuming manner. They were splendid expressions of selflessness, forgiveness, patience and service to others.

Not everyone, however, finds patterns easy to follow. Religious organisations established in the name of a master after their death have often clashed with one another. Interpretations of sacred texts have sometimes been taken too loosely and bitter power conflicts ensued. But at the heart of the original teachings there is much common ground, irrefutable universal truths that can speak to millions through time and space.

Perhaps the hardest of these to grasp fully is that we are all equal. The early masters knew it instinctively, and really did see divinity in every creature, every blade of grass, every drop in the ocean. Their belief in 'oneness' was and is absolute.

For us, however, knowing about oneness, and feeling and understanding it can be two very different things. This was brought home to me in the early days of my spiritual awakening when I was given much gentle direction by a warm and generous healer, Sheila. At the time I was recuperating from a major operation and had gone to Sheila's for help.

One morning as I was lying on her couch with my eyes closed, enjoying the warmth coming through her hands, I became utterly convinced the sun was shining into the room – it was as though it was high summer. I was sure there was bright light all around, but I wanted to double-check so I opened my eyes to take a peek. I realised with shock there were no windows in the room and that the artificial lighting was actually very subdued. I snapped my eyes tight shut again and tried to recapture the luxurious state of relaxation.

As I let my mind drift, I became acutely aware of what I described shortly afterwards to myself as 'unity'. It felt as if Sheila, myself and the Divine were linked together as one being of love.

I cannot recall how long this lasted, but it was probably thirty seconds or more. I noted it as a pleasant, touching experience, not realising that what I was actually being shown was a yawning gap between the spiritual truth of oneness and the reality of how I was expressing it in my own life. If I were honest with myself, I was really only going through the motions now and then.

Let's sidetrack a little further on the concept of oneness and go right back to the very eve of creation to put things into context properly.

Today all major religions have their own version of how the world was brought into being, each person has their own belief system according to the path they walk, and different words – Creator, The Source, Great White Spirit, Big Bang, All That Is, God, Energy, Light, Love, Spirit, Unconsciousness, Mother/Father God… – are used to describe the power that set events in motion.

It does not matter how we express our ideas: go with whatever feels comfortable for you. I will opt here for The Great

Central Sun, since this mirrors the natural world we are so familiar with.

Louise used to enjoy the occasional teasing of one of her colleagues at school, a science teacher called Mike, by asking him very searching questions. These were often of a philosophical nature and, although Mike did not always understand the reason behind the quizzing, he responded to each challenge as best he could.

One morning in between lessons she was pondering the phrase 'as above, so below' which she had come across several times in her reading. She glimpsed Mike in the corridor and sidled up to him, seeing from the look on his face that he was expecting another dive into what he called 'wacky' territory.

With a lovely smile on her face, her enquiry was straightforward: 'If you had to pinpoint the source of all our energy on earth, what would that be?'

He thought for a moment and then replied without hesitation, 'If I had to say only one thing, it would be the sun.'

Eureka! Louise now began to understand what 'as above, so below' means: for everything that happens physically in the world there is a spiritual counterpart, and vice versa. Just as the sun in our solar system provides warmth and light to sustain life, so The Great Central Sun is a cosmic mass of spiritual energy from which we have always derived our spiritual sustenance and, originally, our very core.

Putting it simply, 'in the beginning' The Great Central Sun desired a greater understanding and expanded knowledge of itself. It emanated radiant bursts of brilliant light – the divine blueprint for everything to come and billions and billions of perfect seeds containing the heart of The Sun.

Each of these divine sparks, the essence of perfection and an integral part of the whole, was a soul ready to embark on its own unique, amazing journey of discovery.

Since then all souls, ourselves included, have travelled the universe with a common purpose, gathering riches along the way while preparing for an eventual return to and reunion with the One Source.

The perfect divine plan

Our soul's adventure, or spiritual evolution, unfolds according to a grand plan, and every individual is given plenty of opportunities to learn and implement their part of the plan at their own pace. It is an ongoing process during which certain criteria have to be fulfilled and definite agendas worked through. For example, those choosing to incarnate on earth must, like the masters before them, decide prior to each lifetime which godly qualities they need to explore.

The qualities do not all have to be tackled in one lifetime, although for many on earth it feels as though they have stuck their hands up and said 'I'll take half a dozen together!' They sense an urgency to complete the job properly this time around. But it is not a race, and no one is better than any one else – everything is in perfect divine order and everyone, be they strolling or jogging or sprinting, is doing their best.

Here might be an appropriate place to pause briefly and consider why there is pain and suffering in the world. When faced by the death of a child or a beloved parent's terminal illness even those on a spiritual path may find it difficult to reconcile their beliefs with what they are experiencing.

With much currently taking place on the planet which pushes mankind to the limits, it is hardly surprising that those who have no spiritual leanings often berate a god who allows 'gross atrocities' to happen.

If you find yourself being swept along by bleak news reports, take a step back into calmness and think about this. Every being has the divine gift of free will and every being makes choices before incarnation and during it that weave their own tapestry of life, including how and when the last thread is tied off. All must be respected.

Also bear in mind that when we enter a physical body to play our designated role, which includes paying off karmic debts accrued from previous lifetimes, the veil of forgetfulness descends on us so that we can assume the part with gusto. This means that as we interact with other people (whom we pre-selected at soul level to be part of our life's game), we are marvellous teachers and students for one another.

So, a pernicious dictator might be the instigator of huge changes internationally that ultimately bring about a mass raising of consciousness. And the premature death of a baby might in fact be the working through of a contract between souls who know they have certain lessons to learn before they can evolve further.

However, there is no denying that bereavement for most people is a deeply saddening time – the sense of loss and heartache can be almost overwhelming – and I do not for one moment wish to belittle the grieving process, for it a blessed part of our humanity. If you ever feel torn between how you think you should be reacting in such circumstances and what you are actually doing, ease up on yourself and allow yourself to be the you of the moment. It's a well-worn cliché, but time will eventually put things back in perspective for you, and you will move on with greater strength and compassion. Raw emotions can be transformed to become inner strengths and wisdom.

For the most part remember your divinity and see each challenge in your daily routine for what it really is – a test of your ability to remain in balance at all times. There is no need always to go down the route of pain and distress.

Learning can be fun and a delight, as was originally intended by God. But many people are taken in hook, line and sinker by the illusion of the third dimension and choose time and time again to learn through experiencing pain. Gradually they come to expect nothing else, because they have forgotten that there is another, more joyful way.

Louise was brought to a deeper understanding of third dimensional expectations during the birth of her first child, Alexander. When her contractions started, she did not feel any discomfort in the least and so she convinced herself that they were not really happening – everybody had told her gruesome stories about what to anticipate and this certainly was not it. After a while her husband Andy became concerned about the frequency of the contractions and insisted they get to the hospital as quickly as possible. Still Louise had no pain.

When hospital staff confirmed the baby was on his way, it was only then that she felt herself begin to swim against the natural cosmic flow of events. She consequently tensed her body and by so doing created a resistance which resulted in a forceps delivery and all that that entailed.

A nurse told Louise later that she was a 'natural mother', which confirmed for her that she could indeed have given birth without any painkillers or intervention by doctors. When her next son, Matthew, came along, she made sure she did not take on board an iota of other people's negative beliefs, and there were no hiccoughs of any kind.

Ascension here we come!

The ascended masters are aware of our efforts, and applaud them. They watch with delight as we follow, however hesitantly, in their footsteps, for the only difference between 'us' and 'them' is that they have mastered the physical world through their time spent in human bodies and now they no longer need to incarnate again (although out of love for humanity they can choose to do so). It is said that Buddha incarnated several hundreds of times before finally moving on from the earthly plane.

By remembering who we truly are – a spark from the divine and therefore linked with others in and through love, the essence of The Great Central Sun – and that we have chosen to be here right now, we are ticking off several lessons at once and taking a massive leap forward in consciousness.

Imagine for a moment a car and its headlights and that these represent the body and the soul. Most of us have had many lifetimes acting out an impressive repertoire to allow us to understand every subtle aspect of the qualities mentioned earlier. As a result we have inevitably picked up 'negative' energy along the way, perhaps taken on board from other people or accumulated through neglecting to monitor our own thoughts, actions and emotions.

Anger, guilt, resentment, pain – these can all become locked from past lives into our cell system in this lifetime so that our inner light cannot shine out brightly. This is rather like the dirt and grime a car collects on its travels. Its headlights become dim and need a thorough clean to restore them to optimum brilliance.

The ascended masters have polished their lights, buffed up their bodywork, and are showing us the dripping sponge with bucket of soapy water! By being prepared to roll up our sleeves and get our hands wet, we can really begin to turn our lives around. In other words, after descending into this very dense physical arena, we can reverse that process and step onto our own ascension path out of it. You can, if you wish, stop the cycle of incarnations, and move into a higher state of being as you journey on towards The Great Central Sun. You can become an ascended master too.

What's more, it does not have to be Mission Impossible and you don't need to be perfect – you do not have to be the next Einstein or poet laureate or guru. All it takes is the desire and willingness to achieve your own mastery, and the rest will follow automatically. Simple! And what's more, you can do it in this lifetime.

If you recognise yourself as one of the people putting their hands up for plenty of quality testing and you had not understood why, perhaps you might ponder this now. You might be making sure you don't have to come back here again…

The decision to ascend is made by the soul, because the soul knows who we truly are, what we have experienced so far and what we still need to do. Those used to listening to their inner voice will probably be aware of distant rumblings, though they may not as yet know what these mean, or they may be drawn to find out more about the subject.

Others may not consciously be aware of their soul's choice, but the ascension process will happen for them all the same. It really is an exciting prospect, and especially so if you can observe it taking place day by day.

Support comes, of course, from our guides, angels, the elemental and animal kingdoms, and from the ascended masters themselves – the caretakers of Mother Earth and her inhabitants. In the same way that we must learn and grow spiritually, so they as part of their own evolution have jobs to do, some of which involve overseeing humanity's development.

Indeed it is hardly surprising that people seem inexplicably drawn to a particular master or a group of masters, as they have been with us over many lifetimes, guiding and cheering us on – we have probably chosen to work with at least one of them this lifetime.

Know that if you ask from your heart for their assistance, it will be provided – not always in the way you expect, for then you might not *feel* the experience of your lessons. Believing is one thing; knowing it from within is quite another.

A little extra help from our friends

People often wonder where the ascended masters are. In the Bible Jesus explained the divine organisation in simple visual terms when he said 'In my father's house are many rooms' (John 14, 1). It is a beautifully elegant concept, describing a oneness (the house) that allows for individual spiritual evolution (the rooms).

Today dimensions rather than rooms are more commonly referred to, although there is debate about how many there are – numbers range from single figures to upwards of several thousand. Again, it does not matter whether your image fits with anyone else's, as it is probably beyond most people's ability to describe the arrangement accurately anyway!

Following our motto 'Keep it simple', I will express Louise's and my truths in terms of thirteen dimensions, each vibrating at a different speed, and the thirteenth being The Great Central Sun, God or Source or whatever term you favour. All of us on earth are currently in the third dimension of time, matter and space. When our physical bodies die our soul passes out of time on to the fourth dimension where it recuperates, if necessary, reviews the most recent lifetime, and prepares for the next re-incarnation.

Not needing to experience physicality again, the masters on the other hand have ascended beyond the fourth dimension into higher vibrational dimensions – some people feel there is no precise cut off point between each stage, but a gradual blending from one to another, whereas others sense a 'void' or womb-like darkness between them.

Medieval folk used to talk about the music and harmony of 'the spheres', meaning a constant balance in the heavens even when the world seemed hazardous and chaotic. This is a delightful phrase that evokes angelic choirs, incomparable beauty and peace, and symbolises the realms of ever intensifying light, love and joy where the ascended masters, beings of pure radiant energy, exist. What an incredible picture to think about.

But what is even more remarkable is that we no longer have to gaze wistfully at this view from afar: their world and ours are moving closer together. As Mother Earth starts her own ascension (see page 43), and we continue to purify and literally lighten ourselves as we raise our vibrations, it becomes easier for us to perceive higher dimensional energies when the masters step down their vibrations to match ours.

Throughout this book there are numerous examples of people having experienced direct contact – they have seen breathtakingly exquisite colours, heard voices calling their name, felt the uplifting presence of a high level guide beside them... It is humbling to think we are being cared for so well and that we can ask at any time for assistance, but these incidents also happen for a reason.

Not only are we being given evidence of what can be achieved if we take our ascension seriously, we are also being provided with extra tools and techniques to help us help ourselves – if we are to be masters, we need to be able to cope on our own with anything and everything that crops up.

This book explains how to recognise and use these tools in your daily life – as the saying goes, 'You can do anything if you put your mind to it!' As you gain self-mastery your confidence and abilities will flourish, and so will your relationship with your friends in the higher dominions.

CHAPTER 2

Ascended masters and celestial rays

As well as making some more comments about the ascended masters in general, this chapter will look at the roles of a particular group of seven masters from the seventh dimension and above. They have been known and talked about for decades, and for some people the lofty association of their names with the realms of love and light can send shivers down spines. Nevertheless we can still approach such masters in exactly the same way as we would any other guide or friend – with equal respect, love and… a hearty sense of humour.

Laughter heals and blows away barriers. It creates friendships and reminds us how joyful life can be. It is a glorious gift which many of us, so bound up with studiously doing the right thing, have forgotten how to make the most of. Those in the higher dimensions like nothing better than a good joke, as long as it is not harmful to anyone. They are what you might call masters of playfulness!

I have often been reminded of this when using angel cards for hints on how best to tackle thorny problems. I can guarantee that if I'm taking it all far too seriously I will pick out one of two cards: either the angel dressed as a clown and holding a bunch of party balloons, representing 'humour', or the two angels on a beach kicking a ball around, symbolising 'play'. Whichever it is, it always brings a smile to my face and makes me chuckle.

Names to conjure with

In the levels of light names are not actually terribly important. When you are building a relationship with an ascended master and you ask for their name, you may find it's unforthcoming, does not have what you consider a deeply spiritual ring to it or it changes regularly. For us, what we are called gives a reference point, a way of greeting someone, honouring and caring for them, and thinking about them as an individual. For the masters, although they have travelled along separate learning paths, their experiences and consciousness are united through choosing to exist in oneness. So when we address a single master we are undoubtedly speaking to them all – which is helpful if you can't exactly remember who to call upon in times of greatest need.

Having said that, the ascended masters do appreciate that we like being able to identify between different energies. We are accustomed to looking at one another and distinguishing between our friends, families and acquaintances. It is a natural part of our lives. So those masters who regularly communicate widely with mankind have each adopted names we can be comfortable with. They project aspects of themselves as what we might call personalities, a unique blending of divine attributes we can readily respond to.

It is also well to bear in mind that if you do not immediately recognise a name, it does not mean that you are not connecting with an ascended master – think of all those anonymous, unsung heroes and heroines who quietly balanced themselves and their karma, and mastered their environment. Not everybody has world teacher Sananda coming through!

Always check in with your own heart to discover your truth, as your perception may not be the same as that of the person sitting next to you. One individual might be very visual and in meditation might recognise a master by their twinkling eyes, whereas someone else might be more in tune with their sense of hearing and know that same master by the sound of a gently rippling wind chime. But if you asked both to summarise the essence of the master in question you would probably end up with common elements within the descriptions.

These elements are most noticeable in channelled paintings. The precise details in dress and physical features might vary between the pictures because of the artists' different interpretations – a curl here and a wisp there – but it is clear from the astonishing similarities that every master has their own set of character traits or an energy fingerprint. This, their name and choice of clothing often relate to their last incarnation on earth, although appearance can change depending on circumstances. In their true form – imagine them as pure light of unbelievable brilliance – we would probably be unable to cope with the intensity of their refined energy, so they present every one of us with what we can manage. And that can be a unique, stunning, life-changing experience.

Spot the deliberate mistake

Aside from channelled portraits of the better-known ascended masters, there are countless ways those from the higher dimensions reveal themselves to us. Be alert and look out for anything that is slightly unusual, however apparently small or insignificant.

For instance, there are many people who see pin pricks (and larger) of colour that sparkle briefly in front of or to the side of them, like miniature fireworks exploding in the night sky. A spiritual healer friend, a wise and gifted lady, once explained that these flashes of blue, violet, pink, white, etc are signs from the ascended realms that what you are doing or thinking is in alignment with your higher self or soul. They are little 'Well done!' notes. Those unaware of their significance might dismiss them as tricks of the light or glitches caused by tired eyes instead of enjoying what is intended as a gentle pat on the back.

Another example of a master making an unexpected entrance could have been dismissed just as easily by a group of people travelling together several years ago. They were involved in spiritual work in countries across the world, and part of their mission involved visiting sacred sites to perform various ceremonies.

On this particular occasion the coach had stopped to give the party a breather, and they were looking out over lush French countryside. In the distance they caught sight of an old man wearing tattered clothes and carrying a bundle of sticks.

A few did not give him a second glance, but others sensed something out of the ordinary and continued to observe him as he gradually made his way up the field. When at last he was near enough for them to notice his features, they were moved by his serenity and warm, inviting smile that gave an impression of timelessness. Who was this person they felt so drawn to watch and who suddenly seemed to disappear from sight?

Eventually one member of the group, who works regularly with the ascended masters, said in rather a matter of fact voice that Master Kuthumi had just dropped by. They all marvelled at the suggestion, but it did feel right.

And then they smiled to themselves as they enjoyed the joke – if ever they were to have had the pleasure of meeting Kuthumi in this lifetime, they had expected it would be as some magnificent-looking being bathed in incandescent light. As it was, they could so easily have missed the real fun.

It was a splendid instance of the so-called spiritual hierarchy acting in a typically un-hierarchical way. Master Kuthumi no doubt wished to convey his thanks for all the effort that was going into their enterprise, but assumed the guise of a poor, aged man to do so. And, as always, individuals had to use discernment to verify for themselves whether this was indeed the case.

If ever you are in doubt about an 'event', quietly acknowledge it and say a quick thank you. Even if you think you have invented it, the mere fact that you have opened yourself up to the possibility that something might have occurred will allow it to happen again.

Try also to make a mental note of the circumstances in which you are given an experience – who were you helping, and how? what were your thought processes? You might be able to replicate these in the future and so establish a positive pathway in your brain. Or maybe it is time for you to bring a new quality into your life. Or perhaps the answer to the question you were asking yourself is 'yes'.

It is amazing how a heart-felt idea or thought can bring an almost instantaneous reaction. But don't expect it every time. The more you learn and put into regular practice – the more you achieve self-mastery – the less waving of flags from the side line you need.

Rainbows

Before focusing on the seven ascended masters let's first talk about 'celestial' or 'cosmic rays'. Imagine a large quartz crystal hanging in one of your windows at home on a spring day. With the sun in the right direction, you would probably notice the refracted light as the rays of the rainbow, perhaps glowing on a wall opposite you or making a surprising splash of colour on the floor. This is one of our world's delightful manifestations that depends on the sun and its light.

Following the 'as above, so below' rule, a similar phenomenon happens on the spiritual level. If you could slow the light down enough to see, you would be able to make out twelve cosmic rays – seven 'old' and five 'new' – originating from The Great Central Sun and beaming out into the vastness of creation.

I will talk about the five rays later on (they are so recent and exciting that they merit a chapter on their own) and deal for now with the seven more familiar rays that have been entering our universe for some time. They have different colours from those in the conventional rainbow: they are blue, yellow, pink, white, green, purple and gold, and violet. Each comprises the quintessence of one or more divine attributes, which can be summed up as: protection and the will of God; wisdom; love; purity; healing; devotion; and transmutation.

You may have come across information which suggests there are many more rays than these seven, that the colours are not the same or that the qualities associated with each do not match those outlined here. Early channellings last century certainly implied other ways of describing the celestial rays, but Louise and I feel the changes since then take account of the progress Mother Earth and humanity have made. We are now sufficiently advanced to benefit from an accelerated learning programme to help us take our last few ascension steps to the fifth dimension.

Each of the seven cosmic rays is overseen by an ascended master – a planetary steward also known as a 'chohan' which in Hebrew literally means 'teacher' – and by an archangel. The intensity of the rays, either singly or collectively, can be magnified or, as is often said, 'turned up'. This can be for the earth as a whole, for continents, countries (such as during wars), towns, etc, and even for individuals who may or may not be aware of the rays' regular pulsating rhythms.

Through absorbing them we are periodically given major boosts of energy on special frequencies that will help us, if we so choose, with whatever we must confront and deal with, be it on a physical, mental, emotional or spiritual level. It is believed that these boosts are happening increasingly frequently, and that sometimes their effects can manifest in the body as aches and pains or flu-like symptoms.

At other times the rays are each turned up modestly on a weekly basis, which you can consciously utilise to your advantage. For instance, if you are asked to arrange a business meeting in which you have, say, to give a presentation, and you're feeling nervous about it, Tuesday might be a good day to pick – it's the day when the blue ray, a ray that can amplify strength and courage, is turned up.

The rays also influence us profoundly in other ways. As part of our evolution curriculum our souls decide before each incarnation which ray attributes will play a prominent part in our life. If, for example, you had spent a few lifetimes acting out the role of an ignorant, proud or narrow-minded person, your soul might now decide it was time for you to balance the scales and acquire knowledge, humility or openness. You would then be born with the yellow ray of wisdom dominating your make-up, and yellow type events would be brought to you that would give you opportunities to prove yourself.

Having the ray close to hand, as it were, can obviously be a definite plus factor, but it can also work to your disadvantage if you allow it to push you to extremes and you are not able to achieve that goal of balance. It can therefore be helpful to know your life's contracted ray, as it will give you a good indication of your potential strengths and weaknesses (see Chapter 7, exercise 12, for suggestions on how to establish what your ray is).

As part of taking greater personal responsibility for yourself and what happens to you – and that is what being a master is all about – you can call upon an ascended master or archangel from any ray to aid you with specific tasks. Or you can visualise ray colours round yourself, places or people, or perhaps wear clothes in colours that will bring through the higher vibrations.

Whatever you do, always ask for an outcome that is for the highest good of all concerned, as you may inadvertently be imposing your ego's desires on a close friend or relation and thereby denying them the opportunity of learning a very important lesson. To cover yourself you need only say something along the lines of '*Through Divine Light and Grace*' followed by your request, perhaps '*I call upon… to…*' or, more powerfully for you as a master, '*I command that such and such be done*'. Feel it coming from your heart and soul.

Repeat the same wording twice more, and your petition will be acted upon. Leave it at that and don't keep raking over old ground. If you find it difficult to let go of an issue, think of a whining child – not an image to aspire to!

A woman who had recently been introduced to the idea of working with the rays was driving to an appointment with a clairvoyant healer. She decided that it was about time she gave herself credit for what she had achieved in her life so far and that a little self-loving would not go amiss. So, she imagined a swirling pink cloud enveloping her, the pink ray being that of love. She even tried visualising breathing it into her body and bathing the parts of herself that were giving discomfort, and she then felt foolish because she wondered whether what she was doing would really have any effect. She also found it difficult to see the colour properly in her mind's eye.

After the healing session the healer said, 'Mary, I don't know whether you realised it, but today you have been surrounded by a beautiful deep pink. Someone must be sending you lots of love!' She was naturally shocked by his revelation, but immensely grateful for the confirmation that, although she could not see it herself, what she thought were bumbling attempts at working with the pink ray were nevertheless successful.

Julie, a recently trained hypnotherapist who has been on her spiritual path for some years, often visualises pink around people when she finds herself in awkward situations. An instance she remembers vividly, because of the favourable outcome, happened one evening while she was in her local pub with some friends. A man across the room kept looking at her in a menacing way. She did not return his glare but nor did she shrink inwardly at his hostility. Instead, she mentally surrounded him in a pink bubble and projected this bubble until the atmosphere changed. The dark cloud around the man lifted and from then on, much to everyone's relief, all had an enjoyable night.

If you are a tactile sort of person, you might prefer to work with appropriately coloured crystals, fabrics or textured paper, or if you are drawn to essential oils there are fragrances that are imbued with the rays' essences. By setting the right intent in your mind and, with practice, using your senses – your body's natural abilities – intuitively, there really is no limit to how much the rays can infiltrate every aspect of your life.

It's fun to keep a diary of what you do and when. You might discover patterns emerging, and it's a good way of charting your progress as well as keeping a note of those special incidents. Sometimes their meaning will not become clear for weeks or even months, but you'll enjoy fitting the jig saw pieces together.

The seven chohans and the seven rays

Over the years very wise, deeply spiritual individuals, such as Alice Bailey, Elizabeth and Mark Clare Prophet, Diana Cooper, Beryl Sevior, Sandy Stevenson, Joshua Stone and many more, have brought through invaluable information about the chohans and the rays. This inevitably is an ongoing process, because rays and their personnel are ever changing as beings in all dimensions continue to evolve and grow. Following our own guidance, Louise and I now offer as concisely as we can what for us are up-to-date details. Take from them whatever resonates with you.

If you are drawn to a particular colour or chohan, this may be a sign for you of the divine quality or ray you are here to represent. Some people are working with several rays, so bear that in mind if you respond to more than one.

1 The blue ray

On a glorious summer's day when the sky is that gorgeous azure hue or the sea is a dazzling Prussian blue, spirits soar and you feel vibrantly alive. The uplifting, dynamic combination of light source and vast blueness instils a marvellous sense of wellbeing, almost like experiencing 'heaven on earth'. It is why blue, the colour of the first ray, is often said to be the closest to the Creator or the Will of God. And it is quite apt that the Divine Plan is referred to as a blueprint for the cosmos.

Blue is also associated with the throat chakra (although as you will see in Chapter 5, chakra energies are changing!) and therefore with communication. In its widest sense communication includes crossing between spiritual dimensions – the 'blue doorway' is often referred to as an entrance to psychic realms. Blue is a guiding energy too, as symbolised by some road signs. We may take many turns and detours on our life's journey, yet once we accept what God intends for us we are carried quickly along the main road to our rightful destination.

The blue ray is overseen by ascended master El Morya. One of his incarnations was as a Tibetan Buddhist in the Himalayas where two other ascended masters, Djywal Khul and Kuthumi, lived quite close by. El Morya is commonly shown in paintings wearing a turban, and having penetrating eyes and a luxuriant moustache and beard. It is thought that our soul discusses its plans with him before we incarnate into another lifetime, which might be one of the reasons why many people favour blue or are attracted to the name of El Morya. (It's a point to mull over if you're trying to solve the mystery of your own ray colour – the picture may not be quite as straightforward as you think.) There are some men and women who even have a vague memory of their meeting with the master and others who have flashbacks during meditation. If you wish to reaffirm your connection, you can ask at any time for it to be done.

Some people do not even consciously have to ask! Vicky first became aware of El Morya's presence when she sensed a high vibrational energy around her. She had also frequently been seeing flashes of blue, sometimes with gold, and wondered what it all meant. When she was shown an artist's impression of the ascended master, with a large glittering sapphire at the front of his turban and sparkling sapphire and diamond rings on his fingers, the frisson of recognition that ran down her spine spoke volumes to her. Now having experienced his energy on many occasions, she describes El Morya as a 'firm but very loving' teacher who expects a certain amount of hard work and dedication to tasks in hand.

El Morya is assisted on the first ray by Archangel Michael who is usually depicted with a fabulous cobalt blue cloak and a majestic sword. You can call on either or both of them for protection, courage and strength. Of course you can always imagine yourself clothed in your own invincible cloak instead.

Fortify your resolve by saying in your mind or preferably out loud three times in succession every day, '*I am a Master and according to Divine Will I am now protected/strong/determined to…*'

As with any affirmation, the more you use it, the more powerful it will become. You may not at first believe totally in what you are saying, but what you are doing very effectively is projecting positive energy via your words and voice, and thereby letting the cosmos know exactly what your expectations are. Once the universe has adjusted itself to your new intended energy direction, you will be given every assistance to achieve your goal. You will become what you are decreeing.

I once met a lady whose fine attunement with the angelic realms had brought much harmony into her life. She offered some sound, pragmatic advice about protection for family and friends, a subject probably close to most of us. Instead of sending out a daily prayer, or doing it on an *ad hoc* basis, you can simply ask for a week's cover at a time – something several of us thought was an excellent idea. Tuesday would be an appropriate day to make your request.

On a separate note, red used to be the colour of the first ray. But, as mentioned earlier, humankind's and Mother Earth's requirements have shifted as consciousness has expanded, and the cosmic rainbow's composition has now been altered. Louise, who has worked for many years interpreting people's dreams astonishingly accurately and is regularly given information from the higher dimensions in her own, has received several confirmations of this change. These have reinforced what she has firmly believed and felt in her own heart for some time.

A good example came in response to a question she posed before retiring for bed. This is a useful technique if you are looking for some form of guidance. People find that asking a question before going to sleep, or writing it on a piece of paper – if you try this, be as specific as you can – and putting it under their pillow, can yield helpful answers via the dream state. You may need to learn your own personal code of dream symbols, but in time you will recognise important messages easily.

Without beating about the bush, Louise asked: 'Have the cosmic ray colours changed?' That same night she became aware of a bright red streaming down in front of her. It contained black symbols, representing the 'downloading' of information (see page 124) from The Source which occurs when we absorb the energy of the rays. Gradually the red receded and was replaced by a blue, also strewn with symbols.

After that, no other colours were forthcoming, but the words 'Divine Will' were deeply imprinted on her mind. She took this to mean that, as the new colour of the first ray had been verified, she should accept and trust that her interpretation of the other rays was correct. This understanding is the basis of the information presented throughout this book.

2 The yellow ray

Daffodils and dandelions, buttercups and primroses – bright, uplifting flowers to herald warmth, new life, sunshine and optimism…

If you're ever feeling gloomy, a bunch of golden blooms popped into a vase where you spend much of your day soon works on clearing negativity.

I keep a clutch of curly yellow ribbons dangling on a notice board immediately behind me in my office for the same reason. I might not see them with my eyes, but my body is aware of their presence. I'm also a great fan of sunflowers for the garden. I like to think they are a cheering sight for anybody walking by. Similarly, walls painted yellow in schools' mathematics and science rooms can have an inspirational effect on children.

People naturally drawn to yellow are vibrant and upbeat, and they enjoy making others laugh. Perhaps it is the link with the sun and therefore with God, the everlasting light and our own inner light, that maintains their spirits.

Aura photographs showing large areas of yellow can often signify a dynamic, active mind, since the colour is also associated with knowledge and thinking. These reflect the second ray's virtues of wisdom and vision, qualities mirrored in Lord Lanto's stern-looking but sage countenance. With a white beard and thin white moustache, it is easy to imagine this chohan once a ruler in China and a contemporary of Confucius. Archangel Jophiel assists Lord Lanto on the second ray, and Sunday is a day you could set aside now and then for their contemplation.

3 The pink ray

Nature and her ever-changing array of glorious colours are a constant reminder of spiritual truths. Take cherry trees, for instance, fluffed up with pink blossom in the spring. As they shower their delicate petals onto the ground underneath their weathered trunks, wind and rain soon blow the flowers away. One day they are there, and the next they are gone before you've had time to savour their precious beauty.

In other words, life is for living in the moment. Take your chances while you can and recognise the godliness in all.

The pink ray is the ray of divine and unconditional love, of forgiveness and self-love, which is why painting prison cells with pink makes such sense – the colour seems to help calm violent criminals.

One way of explaining this is that it brings together the opposite ends of the old third dimensional chakra system: the white light of the crown chakra, the link with the divine, and the red energy of the root chakra, the link with the earth. They combine to form a totally different energy vibration, that of compassion. Interestingly, horticulturalists have discovered that pink light promotes health and growth in roses which are themselves symbols of love, tenderness and compassion.

The third ray's chohan is Paul the Venetian, so named after his final incarnation as Paolo Veronese, a famous artist who worked in Venice in the 16th century. Channelled images of him show a determined looking face with strong jaw line and Roman nose. He is said to influence people working in architecture, where sacred geometry can be brought to the fore, and in design, especially these days of cars.

On one of Louise's courses last year a man made an intriguing comment when he pointed out that until the 1960s cars were very akin to boxes on wheels. Then, the likes of Ferrari and Lamborghini began to produce sumptuous models which took the world by storm. What a nice touch that Italy, home to Paolo Veronese, should have been so instrumental in developing what have now become classics.

Chamuel, whose name means 'He who sees God', is the archangel of the third ray. He can be called upon for healing racial tension or if you are having relationship problems. For those who like working on different issues throughout the week, Monday is the day for concentrating on pink ones.

As an aside, the colours of the first, second and third rays symbolise our divine spark or soul. The 'three-fold flame' of divine will, wisdom and love burns unceasingly within our heart centre. You can honour this gift by lighting a trio of appropriately coloured candles and perhaps meditating on them. During workshops Louise will sometimes invite people to dip their hand into a bag and take out, unseen, a blue, yellow or pink tea-light.

Exclamations of surprise at what has been selected can be very illuminating in themselves, and choice of colour can often bring meaningful messages to those who are honest with themselves. Group members then light their own tiny candle from a single taper in acknowledgement of their link with the others in the room and with the supreme Source of all Light. Sitting together, with the little flames flickering brightly round a table, they find the informal ceremony is a lovely way of expressing oneness.

4 The white ray

A bride nervously takes her father's arm and walks softly down the aisle, every guest turning to admire her dress as it rustles by. A priest makes the sign of a cross on a baby's forehead and then holds the child out to his proud mother who reclaims her son, rearranging his robes and settling him into her embrace. Two figures, almost bent double as a keen wind rages against them, taste snow flakes in their mouth and watch the countryside disappear under a blanket of swan down.

What links all these scenarios is of course white, the symbol of purity and cleanliness. For some people white is like the light from which all colour was conceived and to which we travel at the end of our life. For others it is moonlight, a reflection of the sun, which illuminates subconscious thoughts and emotions.

However you think of white, the divine attribute the fourth ray radiates is purity. You are encouraged to heighten this quality in your own life by ascended master Serapis Bey, who guides those who are serious about their ascension path.

One of Serapis Bey's famous incarnations was as pharaoh Amenhotep who through his endeavours brought peace and prosperity to Egypt. Archangel Gabriel, also of the fourth ray, is revered among followers of several religions, including Islam, Judaism and Christianity.

I wonder about the time chosen for Christ's crucifixion which significantly, in terms of the rays, is supposed to have been Friday, the day of the fourth ray of purity.

Only Jesus's unblemished, high vibrational energy prevented him from being overcome by the mass of negativity on earth at the time, thereby allowing him to offset a large portion of humanity's huge karmic debt. It somehow seems appropriate that 'Good Friday' witnessed this momentous event.

5 The green ray

In Dylan Thomas's famous poem 'Fern Hill' he evokes quite brilliantly an idyllic, carefree youth flourishing under the influence of a benign Mother Nature. Innocence, beauty, contentment, and the very act of creation itself are all epitomised by a single word repeated over and over: green.

The poem works well because it strikes a chord with anyone who responds to the natural world. For many people green trees, green leaves, green grass and open spaces all speak of calmness and harmony (in some beliefs the traditional god of nature is called 'The Green Man'). No wonder that organisations committed to ecological causes, to bringing balance back to earth, should adopt the colour and its associations as part of their name. 'Greenpeace' is an obvious example.

It is most appropriate, then, that the quality (qualities are sometimes known as 'virtues') of the fifth ray is healing in all its many forms. Which brings me back to nature again, or more specifically to trees whose roots reach down into the earth and whose branches stretch up towards the light. A comparison with ourselves is never far away – how often are we advised to remain centred and grounded, especially when we are doing spiritual things? And healers are sometimes taught to visualise roots extending from their feet and travelling down into the ground to act as anchors.

As for trees themselves, they obviously heal by providing sub-stances from which drugs are made, but their strong energies do also sooth frayed nerves. I always used to scoff at people who advocate hugging a tree until I tried it for myself. Several years ago I was at rock bottom with chronic illness and, although I didn't really know about spiritual matters then, I told myself that I should start making changes in my life if I was to get myself out of the deep pit I had allowed myself to fall into.

I went out into a nearby field and put my arms around an old oak tree. Placing my cheek against its rough trunk, I felt a warmth against my skin, and I closed my eyes. I was astonished to see what in retrospect I realise were its internal structures – woody arteries and soft tissues, and movement within them. I recoiled instantly in shock because the experience was unnerv-ing. But I now realise this dear tree was sharing with me knowl-edge of the fifth ray to kickstart my own healing journey.

There are two chohans for the green ray: Lord Hilarion and Lady Pallas Athena, a striking, distinguished figure with golden hair. In contrast with the other chohans mentioned so far, Pallas Athena presents a female rather than a male energy. However, this is probably down to personal choice, as all ascended masters have achieved perfect balance between their masculine and fem-inine aspects; the concept of gender is relevant only in that we in our third dimensional reality are accustomed to seeing men and women. It is not uncommon for ascended masters to look like neither and both simultaneously!

In paintings of Hilarion his sense of humour plays around his mouth and eyes. This refreshing energy encourages us to believe in ourselves, and children and young people respond well to its positivity. Julie, the same lady who visualises pink bubbles around people, had never realised until very recently why she has so many tapes about Hilarion, and why most of her house is painted green – it has always been her favourite colour and one to which she is invariably drawn. Before qualifying as a hypno-therapist, she worked for many years with homeless men and women. Both vocations fit under the wide umbrella of healing, and this is probably the reason why she has an affinity (now recognised!) with the fifth ray and its chohan.

Archangel Raphael, the most frequently portrayed angel in western art, can help with fifth ray issues too. Even if you have no experience of giving healing, you can simply request that Raphael (or any angel come to that) work through you. Ask for the highest good for your 'patient' and for yourself, and give thanks for the learning opportunity. Then call on your angel of healing, release any thoughts your ego might be prompting, and allow the process to happen. Trust and just go with what you are intuitively led to do. You may be surprised at the results. I once watched a group of 'non-healers' try this for themselves, and they were amazed at the energy that came through their hands – they didn't necessarily feel it themselves, but their partners on the receiving end certainly did.

6 The purple and gold ray

For centuries gold has stood for power, material wealth, security, success, royalty, religious worship, and exoticism. Golden lions in front of golden gates protected ancient temples, and in the East statues of Buddha were crafted from this precious metal.

Even today pilgrims visiting shrines honour Buddha by rub-bing sheets of gold leaf thin as tissue paper onto the monuments. Gold stars are awarded to children for trying hard at school, and gold medals are given to athletes who have put all their efforts into reaching their physical peak. In short, this 'noble' substance can represent the finest that can be achieved by anyone at any level of ability in any discipline – the warmest compliment you can pay someone who is generous and loving is to say they have 'a heart of gold'. Of course gold has also been associated with greed, overreaching ambition, pride and corruption, the converse of the purple and gold ray's qualities. But it is not gold itself which is at fault, merely people's misuse of it for their own selfish ends, the Biblical 'love of money'. Fortunately, used with integrity, the sixth ray can actually help release desires and fears.

Lady Nada, formerly a priestess in Atlantis, will support anybody who earnestly aspires to be the best they possibly can – try assessing your own set of resolutions on a Thursday. She will reassure you in your quest no matter how many times you falter. If the right intention is there, she and Archangel Uriel will make sure it is nurtured, infusing you with the ray's sacred attributes of service, selflessness and co-operation with others. Like the old alchemists, who also were seekers of knowledge and spiritual truth (represented by the purple on the ray), and who strove to change base metals into gold, so we can perform miracles on ourselves – a major theme in the next few chapters.

I have seen artists' impressions of Lady Nada with long flowing hair and eyes conveying the sort of expression that exhorts you to dig deep within yourself and keep persevering. A large ruby, the precious stone of the sixth ray, glitters from garments about her head and neck. Lady Nada took over from Jesus when his task of overseeing humanity during the Piscean age came to an end. His learning path has since carried him on to the next step of his spiritual evolution where, known as Sananda, he is fulfilling his new role as world teacher.

It's easy to become sidetracked by the different grand-sounding job titles and movements among members of the spiritual hierarchy. Tracing the multi-dimensional branches of the cosmic tree can be fascinating, but it's not essential to learn them all. You might start with the chohans, world teachers Kuthumi, Maitreya and Sananda, and Sanat Kumara, who holds the divine plan for Mother Earth. But it really is up to you – in time you may be led to whoever is important for you anyway, so don't worry if you do not share your earthly friends' enthusiasms. And for some people, just having a general awareness that the ascended realms are in good hands is sufficient for them.

7 The violet ray

The number seven and the colour violet are both connected with magic, mystery and mysticism, an appropriate combination, then, for the cosmic ray of transmutation.

Violet has the shortest wavelength in the conventional colour spectrum and, being of high vibration, can be the most calming – ultraviolet light is used in medicine for the treatment of some cancers and skin conditions, for instance, and in the East it is believed that sleeping between violet sheets will make you live longer, presumably because of the colour's restorative properties. For many, the purple of kings and bishops is a link with the ethereal realms and the ability to see into the unknown, and it is often the first colour people notice appearing in their life after committing themselves to their spiritual path.

Not long ago I heard a lady confess that she had automatically assumed everybody sees violet when they close their eyes until she passed some innocent comment to her husband. He peered at her quizzically, with eyebrows raised to the ceiling, and said, 'Violet? What do you mean, violet?' She then somewhat reluctantly admitted that just before going to sleep, or when she meditates (he wasn't aware of that, either!), this luscious colour bursts onto the scene. He was rather taken aback, but he was also intrigued.

As well as purification and manifestation, the seventh ray's qualities are transmuation and healing (see Chapter 4 on the violet flame for more detailed explanations). These are supervised by Archangel Zadkiel and Saint Germain whose previous incarnations include Roger Bacon (1211-94) and the philosopher Francis Bacon (1561-1626).

Paintings of Saint Germain show a rather dashing, bearded man with piercing eyes – I make no excuse for mentioning eyes, truly gateways to the soul, yet again, for it is the ascended masters' which are their most remarkable, compelling feature.

You can recognise old souls on earth today by their eyes which seem to be illuminated from within. James Twyman, one of the world's great peace makers, has become involved with a group of what have variously been called 'psychic', 'indigo' and 'crystal' children. They are highly evolved beings who have chosen to incarnate at this critical time in our history to offer wisdom and promote harmony. They are spread throughout the world and many of them are severely disabled, but this allows their souls freedom of movement.

Very early on James asked his first contact with the group, a boy called Thomas, how he knew others like him. His answer was that all the children communicate telepathically, and that they have only to look in each other's eyes to see the colour and the light shining through.

Following their example, anyone can connect with another person's soul by briefly holding their gaze, smiling, and acknowledging with love their divine being (some people also visualise sending out light or a colour to whoever they meet in the street). Try it when you're out shopping among strangers and you may be delighted by the response – you can experience a meaningful soul to soul link which might last only a fraction of a second, but it will resonate deep within your heart. If the responses do not always appear positive, don't be put off: your love and light will still have a beneficial effect.

Saint Germain's role as chohan of the violet ray (which is generally turned up considerably all the time at the moment) is to oversee the new Aquarian age for the next two thousand years, a not inconsiderable task but one for which he has countless helpers on the earth plane.

It cannot be stressed too much that, however much the ascended masters are serving humanity, their efforts would be much less effective without our contributions from the physical dimension. It is a two-way, mutually beneficial process, and the more knowledge and information we have of the masters, the better equipped we will be to assist them. (The same is true of the angelic and elemental realms and those who are drawn to work with them.)

Having said that, the real measure of their success will be when we can stand beside them, so to speak, as masters in our own right. The rest of this book is therefore devoted to your ascension and how to use your resources at hand to facilitate and enjoy the experience.

CHAPTER 3

Five new celestial rays

One evening the phone rang. It was Louise. 'Have you seen it?' she asked, her excitement quite palpable on the other end of the line. 'Seen what?' I said cautiously – perhaps the sci-fi pro-gramme I'd thought was on that night had actually been the day before, in which case I'd missed a treat. Louise and I love dis-cussing the metaphysical themes in our favourite sci-fi films: more and more examples of this genre are being made by informed directors intent on spreading spiritual messages.

'The rainbow,' came her quick reply, 'It's bigger…' 'Bigger?' I repeated, still none the wiser. 'Yes, there are more colours… I saw them this morning. There were definitely two extra colours beyond the violet – a turquoisy-blue and a deep pink. And what's even better, some children at school picked them out too!'

I let out a squeal of delight. What wonderful times we live in, we both agreed.

Two weeks later I was able to confirm for myself what Louise and the children had observed. I was out on the moors with my husband, driving in squally weather. The clouds were slate grey and the landscape was periodically darkened by their swooping shadows.

Suddenly the sun gleamed through a crack over the horizon and there, as I glanced to my left, was an extraordinarily wide rainbow. After giving it my full attention, I was thrilled to spot two unusual, unmissable strands of colour which lay next to the purple.

When Louise and I described the rainbows to friends, their astonishment was soon replaced by a barrage of questions: 'How come there are more rays?' and then, 'Well, how many are there – didn't you see just two extra in the rainbows? How do you know? Will we see them?'

They were all good points that needed answering: it hadn't been a trick of the light, as some doubters had suggested, although perhaps in a way it had been!

Here are some of the conclusions Louise and I reached. As happened with the rest of this book, we were blessed with messages and signs from the cosmos which backed up our theories. They did not always come, it seemed to us, in a logical order, but our experiences over several years dovetailed and complemented one another perfectly and with incredible synchronicity. It was as though, after we had been brought together, we were then each shown different perspectives of the same puzzle, and we needed to put our heads together to work out the full extraordinary picture. It wasn't a hardship for either of us and Louise turned out to be amazingly adept at extracting the facts from our mass of spiritual data.

Decision time

Surrounded by familiar scenes that all too often can be taken for granted, it's easy for men and women to forget that Mother Earth is also a spiritual being, learning, evolving and moving towards a reunion with The Great Central Sun. Through expressing unconditional love for all the creatures who have inhabited her kingdom for eons, she has raised her vibration so much that she is now ready, if she wishes, to begin the transition to the next level of her development. And she has indeed chosen her new path: it is the one that will take her beyond the fourth dimension and the astral plane, to the fifth dimension.

But the decision to ascend does not simply rest with Mother Earth. It is crunch time for humanity as well. The dramatic events of 9/11 in 2001, followed by the year 2002, the numerical representation of 'as above, so below', set wheels in motion to prompt every single person to consider which side of the fence they would really like to be on. Everyone must choose imminently, if they have not already done so, either to join Mother Earth's spirit or to remain connected to the physical third dimension, completing further reincarnation cycles until the next opportunity for mass ascension presents itself. There is, of course, no wrong choice, for souls know exactly what is in their best interest.

You might like to try a little exercise to find out how your higher self is playing its cards. Say out loud to yourself twenty times, 'I choose ascension' or, if you're brave enough, 'I choose to ascend to the fifth dimension.' How do you feel? What emotions, if any, does it bring to the surface? There may be a great deal of detritus floating about as negative comments, such as 'I don't really believe this... I'm not good enough... I'm not ready...', but underneath all that does the essence of what you are affirming resonate with you, no matter how faintly, at some level?

Jot any thoughts down on paper and, if you would like some clarification, ask your guides and higher self to show you any barriers you may be putting up to sensing your truth. If you're reading this book, then there is a fair chance your soul has already selected the ascension option and is keen for you to become fully aware of it!

Give yourself time before you try the exercise again, and notice the difference. Don't worry if, after a few attempts over a period of several months, all this continues to sound strange or does not feel right for you. Your soul's preferred choice may be to continue learning through more lifetimes in a physical body. And that in itself will bring rich rewards. On the other hand, if you are warming to the idea of ascension, you can move into alignment with your higher self by decreeing three times *'Through my Divine Higher Self I now choose ascension and, under the Law of Grace, I allow it to happen with ease.'* Your vote is well and truly cast!

Proof positive

You may be wondering how the new rays, with their special group of divine attributes (wonderfully defined by Sandy Stevenson in *The Awakener*), fit in here. Be assured they are serving a number of crucial functions. Not only are they assisting us in our decision-making, they are acting as attention-grabbing signals along the ascension route. They are making us sit up and take note. As the spectacular colours are progressively infiltrating the third dimension and as more and more people are seeing them, often through their spiritual eyes, we are being provided with marvellous proof of our increased rate of vibration and of the existence of higher realms – it is said the fifth dimension is one of colour and sound, and that the five cosmic rays act as a bridge between the fifth and the third dimensions.

How apt, too, that another rainbow should be part of our evidence. According to Denise Linn in her magical book *Signposts: The universe is whispering to you,* a rainbow 'is one of the most universal signs of blessing. [It] blesses your ventures, your relations and you. It is a message from spirit to you that you are going in the right direction and that your path is blessed and guided.' Apply this to Mother Earth, and to yourself and the fantastic road to enlightenment ahead of you, and you may well tingle in anticipation. The other three cosmic rays, incidentally, will become visible in rainbows when we and Mother Earth are even further spiritually advanced.

Lastly, but most importantly, the five rays give us another set of tools for our ascension kit. We can consciously use them in a similar way to the seven older rays, bringing them into our everyday lives in as many imaginative ways as we can create for ourselves. We should also be aware that their influence is being felt subconsciously at a fundamental level in our physical, mental, emotional and spiritual bodies. As people are making great progress with their spiritual spring cleaning, they are gradually drawing down to themselves out of the etheric from the fifth dimension five new chakra energies (see Chapter 5). And the colours initially of these are the same as those of the new rays.

Colours and meanings
8: The aquamarine ray

The aquamarine ray comprises the divine quality of clarity. If you have been through a tough situation that has now been healed, for instance, you will need clarity to see where to go next. In a sense, it is spiritual logic.

I was first introduced to this ray when I had scant knowledge of the spiritual world, and I was totally unprepared for what came like a thunder bolt out of the blue. In true cosmic ray fashion, it was a 'bold as brass' signal I could not possibly miss, one that led me to friendship with Louise and ultimately to the ascended masters. And the rest, as they say, is history.

At the time, I was learning to meditate. I drew the curtains in the room, lit a candle, and settled myself into my seat. I focused on the candle flame for a few seconds and then closed my eyes. Before I had even had chance to go through a body-relaxing routine properly a massive circle appeared on my inner screen. Then the purest colour I had ever seen shone through the circle with the utmost brilliance. The 'aquamarine' had a crystalline quality, and its radiance was so overwhelmingly powerful that I heard myself spluttering involuntarily out loud, 'Oh, that's *incredibly* beautiful'. I could not hold my gaze for very long – I had to take my concentration away to cope with the intensity of the whole experience.

I tried to replicate the scenario the next night, using the same candle and sitting in the same chair, but nothing transpired. Nor the next night; nor the one after that… So, the rational part of me concluded, it must have been a real event.

Using third dimensional frames of reference, the closest comparisons I can make are with traffic lights. The red, amber and green circles are back-lit by powerful light bulbs, which make the luminous colours projected out to the road clearly visible by drivers and pedestrians alike. The five rays are also distinguished by their combination of colour and light source, although in their case it is The Great Central Sun which is responsible for the spectacular luminescence: greater amounts of Source light are mixed with the new rays than with the older ones, mankind having reached the stage where we are now generally much better able to cope with higher vibrational energies striking the planet.

One of the effects of these rays is to accelerate the evolutionary spiral: as individuals work on raising their consciousness, they attract more energy to them which in turn increases their speed of vibration and therefore their ability to utilise even more high frequency cosmic energy. Anybody of a lower vibration who comes into contact with them will be affected positively in some way, even at a subconscious level, and so the spiritual growth of the human race as a whole is moved on in leaps and bounds.

Furthermore Mother Earth's ascension cause is championed too. As she supports us in our endeavours, so we through our spiritual practices radiate more and more love into the universe, the highest vibrational energy which she can draw on to help activate her own 'light body' (see Chapter 6). Working in this synergistic manner deepens our understanding of oneness and, through joint access to the gridwork of light now being established around ourselves and the planet (again, see Chapter 6 for more on this), allows all of us access to greater levels of wisdom and knowledge.

Louise witnessed a very special event several years ago which illustrates this interconnectedness of spirit and matter, of Mother Earth and humanity at an important stage of our joint evolution, and the major influence of celestial rays on our development.

1999 for Britain was the year of the total eclipse of the sun, a comparatively rare astronomical conjunction when the moon passes between the sun and the earth, casting a shadow on the latter. This shadow, or 'area of totality', is about 65 miles wide and on 11 August 1999 was due to pass over the tip of the south west of the country, very close to where Louise and I live. Even though there was heavy cloud about on the day, she wanted to watch as much of the phenomenon as she could. She positioned herself with her family in a quiet location overlooking the Atlantic Ocean, on the edge of a cliff just outside her local town.

As she scanned the horizon, she could make out a mass of darkness travelling at immense speed. The sky turned a charcoal colour, the birds stopped their chattering, and an expectant cool stillness descended all around.

Then her breath was nearly taken away by the sight of the violet ray preceding the shadow, sweeping from the heavens down over the coast and land – even the sea changed from its usual sparkling blue to a deep violet. The ray was transmuting everything in its path in preparation for the eclipse or, in spiritual terms, the downloading of celestial codes into earth's magnetic grid.

Louise's sister, who was standing with her and who up to that point had not been at all spiritually aware, also experienced something miraculous. Like Louise, she saw the violet ray, but in addition to that she was shown the face of St Germain and was overwhelmed by a feeling of unconditional love which flooded her being. The mystical sequence of events transformed her and her husband's lives, and they are now well and truly on their paths to enlightenment.

But that wasn't the end of it.

After the violet came the eighth ray hot on its heels just a split second before the actual eclipse at 11.11 am (numerologically speaking, a significant moment: '11' is a 'master' number which, among other things, magnifies inherent virtues). From a spiritual viewpoint, this also seemed to make absolute sense. With new information freshly available to us via the grid of light (see Chapter 6), we need to be clear about how and when to use it: clarity of purpose maintained through right action is essential. The aquamarine ray provided an influx of appropriate energy to set up the correct resonances for this to happen.

Louise felt immensely humbled to have been given an insight into these divine mechanisms that are constantly in motion, but which we often only see when their impact on us is going to be the greatest – we can file the memory away and recall it at a later date, perhaps when conveying to other people messages of considerable import.

There has been some debate over whether the five new rays are supervised by chohans. Louise and I feel that currently there are not – here are a couple of other possibilities to consider. Firstly, in recognition of our achievement as ascended masters in waiting, vacancies may be being held open until those who have been selected for the jobs have completed their incarnation on earth this time around. After all, until the veil of forgetfulness is lifted from us when we die, none of us really knows what we have done in our past lives and precisely what stage we have reached in our spiritual evolution. We are, as Leonardo da Vinci's famously coined phrase so rightly puts it, spiritual beings having a human experience. It is also most probable that some men and women have already reached the fifth dimension in previous lifetimes, but they have chosen to incarnate again now as teachers in service to human-ity. A few of them may be destined to become new chohans.

Secondly, perhaps it is The Source itself which is currently directing the rays. As we fully acknowledge our abilities and accept our own mastery, and as we move in greater harmony with our soul and its desires, do we need always to call on intermediaries? If you put yourself to the test a little, you might be surprised at just what you can do. And that includes invoking the new cosmic rays. Following the same protocol as mentioned before – '*Through Divine Light and Grace, I invoke XX to XX…*' – is simple and effective.

If you feel happier with a bit of back up, you can always call on any ascended master to lend a hand. You don't have to do it all on your own but, for those who would like to stretch their wings a little, the opportunity to learn and expand many-fold is there for the taking.

Aquamarine, described very aptly by one person as 'like being in the sea and looking up through the water at the sun', has been noticed in many other situations – flashing around cars in heavy rain, as a thin beam shining down on people's heads (a close friend was going through a difficult time when this happened to her, and would have benefited from a clearer perception of her challenges), as blocks of colour on walls, and so on. It would be nice to think that some souls may already be taking the initiative and bringing the new rays into the physical dimension at appropriate moments.

On the other hand, if you prefer the idea of an ascended master or an angel being part of the activity, you might feel they are the instruments responsible. And that is fine. There is no definitive explanation to suit everyone: the more spiritually aware you become, the more you will experience your own vision and your own truth. You will, as God intended, be a unique co-creator with the Divine, for we are indeed as so often said like individual facets of a perfect diamond, each reflecting light in our own special way.

9: The magenta ray

The ninth ray is imbued with the holy attributes of harmony and balance. It is a prerequisite of ascension that we be completely at ease with ourselves and all those with whom we come into contact. For most people it is rarely achievable every second of every day, because we allow someone or some thing to disturb our equilibrium. But there are many techniques we can learn which, if followed with sufficient determination, can bring enormous dividends. You may already have your own arsenal, but for those who do not or who would like to try something different I offer a suggestion here which I have found works wonders. It is an adaptation of a spiritual nugget I discovered among a set of beautiful aboriginal mandala cards Louise has at home.

Whenever you encounter a stressful situation or feel provoked by another person, don't let things fester for even a second. Straight away imagine yourself stepping out through a door – it could be your front door at home or maybe your own movie star's dressing room door with a string of lights around your name – and into a dimension of pure light. It is where you, in all your glorious radiance, naturally belong.

Visualise yourself as a perfect being, perhaps shed of its physical body, with expanded consciousness and with the ability to see the higher perspective. You are full of unconditional love and recognise the godliness in all that is happening on the other side of the door. You are able to step back from what is bothering you, shower it with light or a ray colour of your choice, and see only its divine purpose. You might also say something like, '*I am a child of God. I am at one with all. I see the best in everyone and every situation that comes into my life.*'

The key to this visualisation is being able mentally to detach yourself from the third dimensional stimulus and to tap in to your higher wisdom. The more you can feel and know that you are indeed a master, or at the very least a perfect, loving being removed from the limitations of your current lifetime, the greater this technique's effect. You can also use this method when you are exasperated by your own behaviour. First of all acknowledge what you don't like about yourself, for it is part of you, and then allow your divine self to flood your mind and body with glittering light that zaps any thoughts or emotions that are not of the highest vibration.

If you are not particularly good at visualising, have a go at thinking laterally to come up with a solution tailor-made to your personality. For example, if you respond to music, you might put yourself among a choir of angels when your red buttons are pushed. You could envelop your problems with your favourite, most uplifting melodies and feel them being washed away by waves of sound.

Whatever you choose to do, an immediate response is essential. Hesitation allows the rational mind to take a hold and emotions to gather momentum. With practice, you will not need to be as strict with yourself, because you will automatically behave as a master – you will always view life from a higher plane.

If you reach a stage where you think your ploys do not seem to be producing results, however hard you try, that's the time to call on the ascended masters. They will give you that little extra support you need to get you over what is like an awkward hump of earth on your path. The hillock is actually an excellent signal, if you did but know it, that you are a hair's breadth away from achieving your goal. By digging a fraction deeper into your inner resources the energy shift you have been working so hard to bring about will happen.

The colour of the ninth ray is magenta, a lovely deep fuschia pink, and it often seems to be around when troubled waters are to be calmed. A few years ago the British farmers were devastated by 'foot and mouth' (called 'hoof and mouth' in the USA), a highly infectious cattle disease dreaded by landowners. The containment measures brought in to combat it were far-reaching, with mass cullings of animals provoking raw emotion among country folk.

At around the spring equinox Louise once again watched the violet and aquamarine rays as they swept across the countryside, cleansing the land and dissipating the gloom around those adversely affected by the destruction of their livestock and, in some cases, their livelihoods.

While many farmers ceased trading altogether and were able to turn to alternative professions, there were others who in the thick of it were certain they would receive little or no financial compensation. The possibility of conflict was never far away. It therefore came as no surprise to Louise when, shortly after the violet and aquamarine rays had left the scene, she noticed 'pools of magenta' over her neighbourhood. The ninth ray was undoubtedly acting as a calming, restorative influence.

Magenta and aquamarine in the rainbow are another confirmation that we are fulfilling our missions. There is much that has to be taken on trust when following a spiritual path and there are times when you could be forgiven for letting doubt creep in and wondering if you are having any effect. But the proof is right out there. Keep going, and keep trusting – you have only to look at today's clothes and fashion accessories, backdrops in television studios and films, cars and wrapping papers, to know that the fifth dimension is close by: its colours, being channelled by designers, are infiltrating our lives at every level.

10: The gold ray

The tenth ray cultivates eternal peace, meaning peace within ourselves. When thinking about this aspect, one man fondly remembered his time spent in the Middle East. His most vivid memories were of towns suffused with a golden light at night. The magical effect created a very tranquil atmosphere for him which he can now return to whenever he goes back to the scenes in his mind.

Serenity will be a natural by-product of achieving mastery of all aspects of ourselves. And that involves living from the heart centre, discerning from moment to moment what feels right for you to do. Discernment is not as tricky as it might appear if you use all your senses and follow your intuition. Louise once ignored this rule and let her rational mind interfere at a critical moment.

She was taking part in a spiritual ceremony which involved people being downloaded with information from a specially coded crystal. She had been told by the highest authority known to her at the time – a lady working directly with the ascended masters who had instigated the exercise – that the downloading should take no more than nine minutes.

Louise's role was, as she thought initially, to provide the crystal and her time for anyone who felt drawn to the experience. However, she soon discovered that she could contribute much more than this simple service. Whenever she placed the crystal in a person's hands and withdrew a short distance to give them some space, she found herself watching inter-dimensional manifestations through her spiritual eyes.

Respecting people's right to privacy, specific details of these have been conveyed only to the individuals concerned. But I don't think she would be giving anything away if I said that over the years she has witnessed swathes of colour – violet, green, pink, aquamarine, silver, gold… – washing over the crystal holders; outlines of guides and other highly evolved beings, including angels and ascended masters, appearing and disappearing; old souls superimposing themselves over faces; birds, reptiles…

The list is long and remarkable, but Louise realises it is not just an awesome show for her benefit! Proof of the downloading process and of other dimensions, as well as personal feedback of a deeply spiritual nature, provide people with unexpected insights which often break open heavily bolted doors for them.

A few months after Louise had started to use the crystal, a woman came to her for a downloading. They went through the usual formalities and Louise sat back in her chair to observe. After the allotted nine minutes had passed, streams of colours were still pouring down through the lady's crown chakra. But because Louise had been told by someone she respected and trusted implicitly that no downloading would take longer, she brought the session to a close.

Afterwards, when she was talking through the implications of what had happened, the woman looked at her and said, 'I felt as though things hadn't actually finished and that there was more to come.' Bingo! If Louise had followed what her instincts were telling her, instead of letting that nagging little voice of mental authority butt in, the downloading would have been allowed to reach its natural conclusion.

Since then Louise has never knowingly let anyone, however well informed or esteemed, prevent her from doing what she feels is right. That is an important lesson for us all: mastery is about making a decision from the heart and standing firm. Don't be swayed by anything or anyone, no matter how impeccable their credentials. Keep your feathers unruffled and peace will always be with you.

11: The peach ray

'Life is peaches and cream!' goes some way to explaining what the eleventh ray is all about, but the true essence of this cosmic gift is much, much more. It combines the two attributes of divine purpose and joy, joy perhaps increasingly coming to the fore as we recognise why we are here on earth. There are, however, many people who have not yet worked out what their mission is and are perturbed by this. They try to elicit clues from the universe to point them in the right direction when in some cases the answer might be staring them right in the face.

If you're wondering what you *should* be doing, stop. The best course of action is to forget about your mission and allow it to reveal itself in its own good time. If you don't like that idea, invoke the eleventh ray and imagine it infusing every cell of your body. Run through your skills and attributes. What are you good at? What gives you enjoyment and makes you feel alive? You probably already have the tools you need for your mission without having to go in search of different ones.

Next, what are your expectations? Be honest with yourself. Take out any ideas your ego might be suggesting, and see whether what is left ties in with the abilities you have already (there's always scope for gaining a few extras as you go along, but that will happen when you really need them).

Is there a huge mismatch or are you gradually whittling possibilities down to a couple of probabilities? If the former, you may suddenly be drawn to a dramatic change in your life requiring you to learn a whole batch of new skills, but in the likely event it does not materialise for you you may have to go back to the drawing board. Don't fret, but treat yourself lovingly – you do have a purpose, a very important one. Relax into the flow of life, and you will be taken to it.

A local woman asked herself these same questions when she was doing some spiritual self-assessment. She analysed herself carefully only to discover her life's purpose was actually much closer to home than she had ever thought possible. She is happily fulfilling her mission through her job as a shop assistant. When customers pack their bags and pay for their goods at her check-out, she has time to chat to them and has got to know some of them quite well.

More often than not she finds herself giving brief counselling sessions, suggesting complementary therapists for people to try, and generally smiling and laughing to raise their spirits. Her work brings her much joy because she is doing her best for others by just being true to herself and her talents. Of course, what she is really doing is expressing in a practical way unconditional love, and unconditional love is the true key to our missions.

The celestial rainbow

Ray	Colour	Chohan/Quality
1	Blue	El Morya
2	Yellow	Lord Lanto
3	Pink	Paul the Venetian
4	White	Serapis Bey
5	Green	Hilarion and Pallas Athena
6	Purple and gold	Lady Nada
7	Violet	St Germain
8	Aquamarine	Clarity
9	Magenta	Harmony/balance
10	Gold	Eternal peace
11	Peach	Divine purpose and joy
12	Opalescence	Transformation

12: The opalescent ray

The twelfth ray of transformation is rather like the lovely irides-cent hues found in an oyster shell's inner mother-of-pearl layer. A workshop member described it quite poetically when she recalled her childhood and how the morning sun would shine through frost on the inside of her bedroom window.

The opalescent ray is the ultimate acknowledgement of our ascension path, for we are but a breath away from realising our intrinsic magnificence. With the help of this cosmic gift, we can be confident about making the transition to master.

Part of the ascension process means welcoming opportuni-ties to expand our consciousness and embracing them as best we can. At one of her talks Louise met a lady who introduced her-self as a medium, although she added hastily that on this partic-ular occasion she would not let her mediumship interfere, as she was there to listen and learn. After Louise had finished speaking, the woman went up to her and thanked her for so many revela-tions.

She explained that when she first started to see energy it was in the form of colours. She did not understand what was hap-pening, but guessed enough to know there was a reason for it and that she should try to develop her gift. The only safe place she felt able to go was a spiritualist church nearby.

The woman quickly became involved in a development circle and almost immediately stopped seeing the colours. Instead, her psychic clairvoyance was brought to the fore, and from then on she became what might be called a traditional spiritual medium, connecting visually with souls in the fourth dimension.

She went on to describe how recently she had felt the need to pull away from the church because of a strong inner knowing telling her it was time to move on. But not quite sure where to turn next, she had spent many hours meditating on her own, while surrounded by pieces of material in all the colours of the rainbow. Slowly, but surely, she was starting to access, among others, fifth-dimensional colours rather than seeing the conven-tional human form of recent years.

Now bowled over by Louise's comments about the celestial rays, this lady was heading straight out to buy material to match all twelve, trusting instinctively that they, and the use of sound, are to play a large part in her future. She has never stopped questioning events in her life and has always been prepared to explore new possibilities to find answers, some of which are proving transformational.

As an aside, it's an exciting thought that we have broadened our horizons so much that it is now possible for people not only to see from the third to the fourth dimension, but to the fifth too. Just as mediums bravely spoke out in the past to present evidence of life after death, we can once more break the mould to bring proof of yet further wonders. And by so doing, others are given permission to acknowledge and broadcast their own fantastic experiences.

CHAPTER 4

The power of the violet flame

All is energy

I would like to start this chapter with a quote from Dr Brian Weiss, an American psychiatrist whose outstanding, ground-breaking work has brought him into contact with people who, when regressed through hypnosis, can recall life in between lives – in other words what souls do when they are not in the physical third dimension.

Enthralling accounts from hundreds of individuals who do not know each other and have never met are so similar that Dr Weiss is convinced these constitute compelling proof of our continual spiritual evolution.

At one point in *Messages from the Masters: Tapping into the Power of Love*, a book chronicling his own mind-expanding experiences with regressed patients, he makes the following comment: 'It is not far-fetched to imagine that there is only one pure energy, that which we call love. As its vibration is diminished, its state changes. We are the solid form.'

This is an excellent way of describing the make-up of the cosmos: everything originally emanated (and continues to do so) from The Great Central Sun, a source of complete, unconditional love. This love does not exist in isolation in a vacuum. It permeates every atom in the universe; in fact it is every atom, although it may be easier to think of it as an energy of the highest vibration, perfect light or infinite knowledge that constantly flows between God and creation. The further we are from The Sun, the denser, heavier and more sluggish it and therefore we become.

If we are not careful our cells, which are made up from and contain this divine energy, can become clogged by pollution, either physical and/or spiritual (for example, by habitually thinking negative thoughts about ourselves and other people). This has the effect of reducing the amount of light or high love energy we can carry and slows our rate of vibration even further.

As I have already explained, preparing for ascension involves taking measures to increase our ability to hold and radiate more and more unconditional love. By ridding yourself of your dirt and soot, you can substantially lighten your load and feel your vibration beginning to accelerate.

You've probably already had an inkling of this whenever you have reacted to another's plight from your heart centre. After taking care of someone else and not thinking for one moment about yourself, you may feel warm inside and have a spring in your step as though a few weights have been lifted from your shoulders. Imagine every day being like this!

The harder you work on yourself, the easier it will become for you to create for yourself whatever you desire. Allow yourself plenty of time, if you need it, to reach your goals and don't try to set yourself too many tasks at once or you may end up being overburdened and unable to master any one properly. You can call upon your higher self and/or the ascended realms to help you work out priorities that will be gentle on you.

Don't worry if on some days everything seems a breeze while on others your inner demons appear at every opportunity. Life is like a swinging pendulum, constantly moving from one extreme to another. The trick is to reduce the impact of the sway on yourself as far as you can.

You can do this simply by recognising and accepting the cosmic law of rhythm, and by not reacting with excessive emotion to your challenges. Gradually you will find the swing diminishes to a small, calm oscillation.

On those days when the darker side of you is brought to the surface, merely thank the universe for giving you the opportunity to transform it and carry on as usual, being especially loving towards yourself and others.

You may also like to remind yourself of the properties of the seventh ray, because it could be just what you need to smooth out those stubborn wrinkles.

The gift of transmutation

We have at our disposal an indispensable aid which transmutes low vibrational energy that may be within us, including our nagging, provocative thoughts, and around us in the environment. As described in Chapters 2 and 3, any of the cosmic rays can be invoked for assistance with specific issues, but it is the violet ray that is particularly effective at dealing with purification and healing on all levels and in literally any circumstance – from removing mental barriers to cleansing places where dark actions have occurred.

Since it is the spiritual equivalent of a third dimensional fire, the ray is often referred to as the 'violet flame'. This pictorial phrase also makes it easy for people to visualise in different sizes – you might see a small version burning in your heart or you might imagine a larger flame engulfing your house; one friend imagines a massive ring on a gigantic gas cooker whooshing into action when she needs it. Or you could shrink your house down to matchbox size and surround that with the violet fire. This technique works well when you're trying to get your mind round huge entities such as countries, continents or even the planet itself.

Louise has spent many years under the wing of St Germain, chohan of the seventh ray, and invokes the violet flame at every opportune moment, often avoiding sticky incidents by doing so. I once asked her how she knows she is working with this particular ascended master. She first described some peculiar experiences several years ago while driving her car – a nice irony, as the car can often symbolise our own physical body.

The windscreen and area behind it would suddenly be filled with a violet colour. Then, on two separate occasions, a flash of electric violet streaked across the dashboard. She interpreted this as a means of attracting her attention and so slowed down. Both times she narrowly missed what could have been a fatal accident if she had continued at her original speed. She now has a sense of protection wherever she goes, and since the car incidents has never been afraid even in potentially dangerous situations.

On a trip to London, for instance, she was sitting on a train at about 8.30 in the evening when a young man leapt on board and crouched down by the seat opposite her. Within seconds a group of unruly youths, who had been slashing seats in other carriages, appeared, closely followed by two railway policemen.

Straight away Louise invoked the violet flame, in her mind flooding the train and its few passengers with the transmuting energy. If the teenagers had so decided, they could easily have crossed that fine line between chaos and harmony and overpowered the police, the crouching man and Louise herself. But in the event the complete opposite happened.

It was as if time was momentarily suspended before the atmosphere in the compartment changed entirely. The young men looked at one another, agreed that they should get off the train and hurried out quietly at the next stop. The policemen also vanished, leaving Louise and the youth, who made his exit shortly after, safe and unhurt.

Louise's next account describes a very moving experience which confirmed for her beyond any shadow of a doubt her link with St Germain. Until then, she had all but denied the relationship, perhaps understandably going into 'negative ego' because of what she believed others would say or think if she were to admit it publicly. She had not yet embraced fully the fact that there is no reason why anyone cannot work with an ascended master, as long as their intentions are right and they do not become pumped up with grandiose feelings or, at the other extreme, overawed by the whole idea. We are as special as the next person and, as masters ourselves, on an equal footing with our enlightened neighbours next door in other dimensions.

Louise was on a course during which various ascended masters, including those associated with the seven cosmic rays, were invited to drop by. As soon as St Germain's name was called, she was filled with blissful, unconditional love which sent tingling sensations rippling down her back. The sheer joy and depth of feeling provoked floods of tears which she could not contain.

Mention such unconditional love in some circles and people will look vacantly at you or squirm in their seats. It is often talked about in terms of what parents feel for their children or lovers for each other. That experienced by individuals meeting with a light being from a high dimension is difficult to describe in words. It is a merging of these emotions, plus much much more – the essences of every pure, nurturing relationship combination you can possibly imagine seem to be blended together.

Once you have felt an ascended master's unconditional love, which is rather like a snapshot of the Divine, you will never forget it. And you will almost certainly recognise it, even if it is less intense, whenever you come across it again. This can be helpful in situations, perhaps during meditation, when you are trying to ascertain whether a being is of a high vibration.

Forgiving endlessly and giving our human rendition of unconditional love to every single person we meet each day is a tall order which few of us will achieve while in a physical body. But as masters on earth we must try – as a wise friend and teacher once told me, 'the way to spiritual growth is love, love, love'.

Going back to Louise's story, she felt a tremendously powerful sense of connectedness. As soon as she accepted it, the link with St Germain became even stronger and she had, and continues to have, innumerable encounters with violet energy. As yet, she has not heard a voice, but feelings and knowingness tell her when and how she needs to act.

In summary: none of us should ever underestimate the astounding properties of the violet flame and you do not have to be contracted with St Germain to use it, although you can obviously call on him and Archangel Zadkiel to help you. If you want to change your life, remember that the flame is an alchemical fire which will transform you back to the golden light of your genesis. It is little wonder that many people begin to see violet, often when meditating, after they make that all-important decision to lead a more spiritual way of life: transmutation has already begun without them necessarily knowing or understanding it.

You might at this point turn to page 161 and to the powerful image digital artist Graham Cheater channelled from St Germain when he asked to '"see" the Master in a way that fits my work, his essence and colours and energy; also in a way that will touch those who look upon it.' This striking picture contains symbols and colours that will act upon you at a deep level. Enjoy its beauty and use it, if you so choose, in your spiritual work.

How to use the violet flame

Protection

There are debates about whether we should invoke some sort of protection for ourselves at the start of the day or just before embarking on any spiritual work. In fact we are more likely to think about our friends' and family's safekeeping than our own. Without buying into fear, it is true to say there are darker forces at liberty in the universe, and so it is prudent to look after ourselves and to make protection a natural part of our daily routine. It's a way of honouring ourselves as well.

Low vibrational elements constitute enormous opportunities for spiritual growth: the brighter you shine, the greater your pull on them – like moths attracted to a lamp – and therefore the greater your achievements when you deal with them successfully, even if you are not really aware of them.

By always following your heart and selecting to walk with integrity the path of light, you will draw in vast influxes of positive spiritual energy which will help to combat negative influences. Not only is that a major contribution to the wellbeing of the planet, it also has a beneficial effect on your own spiritual evolution.

If you do not already have an appropriate prayer, you might like to use the following simple invocation:

I now call upon my Divine Higher Self and Archangel Michael to surround me with Light and Love, and to protect me throughout this day and night. I thank you and trust that this is so.

Say this three times before you get out of bed in the morning and you will be set up for the rest of the day. If you find it difficult to remember words, as an alternative you could imagine walking out onto a stage and into a spotlight. See yourself bathed from top to toe in the shaft of light.

To increase the effectiveness of a visualisation, you could add a few imagined noises to the scene. In this case you could think about a huge switch being turned on for the spotlight and a hum of electricity buzzing round you as the protective shield of light is established. (Remember that white, blue or golden light are for protecting and violet is for purifying, healing and change.) The most important aspect of this exercise, however, is your intent. It does not really matter how you ask for protection, as long as you do. Then trust that all events which transpire will be according to divine will.

Some people use the evenings rather than mornings for contemplation and prayer, in which case an adaptation of the invocation could be used earlier in the day before healing, meditation or channelling. You could say, '*I call upon my Divine Higher Self and Archangel Michael to protect me now with Light and Love. I thank you and trust that it is so.*'

Violet flame invocation

With protection established, you can now move on to the violet flame invocation. Louise and I have found that preceding it with '*I AM a Master*' enhances its effectiveness. This phrase followed, ideally, by the violet flame invocation is so empowering and inspiring (see my second aura photograph on page 166) that it can be said before any affirmation, prayer or action. The first two words are not just in capital letters for emphasis: they also represent our 'I AM presence' or higher self or soul, and the state of perfection we seek in which our mind, body and emotions are all in perfect alignment with it.

Gladys was experiencing problems with her throat which doctors could not alleviate. Her throat had always been a nuisance to her, perhaps because of some past trauma she was carrying over from a former life – during a development session with Louise, Louise saw what she took to be a Frenchman's face superimpose itself over Gladys's, and they later wondered whether she might have been guillotined in a previous incarnation. She also hated eating in front of others and found chewing difficult.

During the night she would often need to have a drink of water, so each time she did so she took the opportunity of saying beforehand, 'I AM a Master. I now heal my throat.' Gradually, over several months her condition improved substantially and her self-belief in her own healing abilities blossomed.

If at any time you reach an impasse with your own health issues, try including the word 'allow' in your affirmations, such as '*I now ALLOW myself to be healed completely in mind, body and spirit.*' It might seem a pedantic alteration, but it will encourage that minuscule part of you that may be sabotaging all your good work to come on board.

The violet flame can be used in any number of ways and is invoked by saying the following three times:

I AM a Master. Through Divine Light and Grace I now invoke the Violet Flame to transmute the energies in and around [me/the planet/name of person/place, etc] and to transform them into Light. Let it be so. So it is.

Fill in whatever is appropriate for you in the square brackets – you can be as specific or as general as you wish. You will probably notice a gathering of strength in your inner and/or outer voice as the words begin to vitalise you and the violet flame is brought into action. Look at the middle photograph in Louise's sequence of aura photographs on page 167 to see just how effective the invocation is.

If the wording does not suit you, tinker with it until it feels comfortable for you. I will often use a shortened version or a simple, quick visualisation during the day, but to compensate for this, however, I usually ask first thing in the morning that the highest good should be the outcome of all requests I make that day. On waking I say something like: '*I AM a Master. Through my I AM presence I today invoke the violet flame for my highest good and for the highest good of all.*' That makes life easier *and* covers me!

If you prefer not to use an invocation, you can summon up a feeling or a word you associate with the violet flame. Or you can just visualise the flame swirling round the focus of your attention. This is handy when there is either insufficient or too much time in the equation.

You might be rushing to an appointment and have only a few minutes to reach your destination. On the way you might come across a homeless person looking rather ill, sitting in the street. Unable to do very much on a physical level, you could nevertheless imagine violet around his or her body.

Alternatively, you might be on a long journey, passing through towns and countryside, accident hot spots and damaged roadways. In those circumstances you could visualise a stream of violet billowing out from your car, motorbike or train and covering the landscape. Once you had set up the image in your mind, you could then ask St Germain to keep the flow of energy going for as long as you were travelling.

It's unlikely you would be able to hold your concentration on violet flame activity for a long period, especially if you were driving, but you could still tap into it now and then to give it a boost.

Seeing the violet flame

If you actually see violet (or any purple or lilac hue – the precise depth of colour will be appropriate to you and the situation) when you are working in this way, all well and good. But you may also find yourself coming across it at other times. When this happens, stop for a moment and ask why. There is always a reason and you may be able to help someone.

During one of Louise's adult education courses she and another lady were working together on an unrelated exercise. As Louise looked at the woman's face, a small violet energy appeared to the left of her head.

Having established on previous occasions that size often relates to the 'type' of being present (an archangel, for instance, will usually be enormous!), Louise gently asked her partner whether she had any connection with a baby or child no longer in physical form.

The lady was greatly moved by this question and, relieved to hear about her lost child, burst into tears. As she has a fear of spiritualist churches, it was an opportune moment for her to receive healing through confirmation in a different setting of the continuation of life after death. The incident could also be viewed as another pointer to the fifth dimension – the child did not come as a traditional fourth-dimensional presence, but rather as pure coloured energy we now associate with the higher dimension.

I had a similar experience when visiting an acquaintance whose work involves past life therapy. While we were sitting chatting, a mass of deep violet flashed from the window to the fireplace where for a brief second it stood about 1.5 metres high. Leighton detected I was slightly taken aback by something in the room and asked me about it. Knowing he would not be fazed, I told him what I had seen.

His face lit up and he wondered whether it could have been the energy of his wife. Unbeknown to me, she had been a very spiritual lady, a gifted healer, and had died several years previously.

Up to that moment I had never given much thought to the colours I am often shown, but had just enjoyed the show. I then realised I needed to be more discerning and proactive, always ready to tune in to messages from the universe. They can teach us a great deal if we are open to them, even though we may not always understand them fully at the time.

Lucille, who attended one of Louise's workshops about the celestial rays, wrote to her several days afterwards, making these observations: '… since the weekend I have been seeing more and more violet light… in strange places – my husband's hand, a lamp post, and one day a big sheet of it across my lounge. Fascinating!!' She is now taking positive steps to understand and utilise this amazing new phenomenon that has entered her life so dramatically.

What is even more important is that she has the courage to speak out to others – the 'violet light' might indeed seem to be in 'strange places', but what that is telling us is there is no aspect of our lives, however mundane, that cannot be affected. You have permission to acknowledge to yourself and others what you might currently be dismissing as sheer fancy.

If you never catch sight of the violet flame, still know that it is working for you. At a large 'new age' festival last year, a woman was attracted to a crystal wand on display on one of the stalls. She picked it up and sensed its energy to be very strong. After she put it back on the table, she felt queasy and instinctively knew she should cleanse herself (you can never tell what problems people may have had who have handled an object before you).

Still feeling nauseous, she made her way to Louise's stand and asked for help. Louise suggested she invoke the violet flame, which she did immediately. Sitting at the side of a crowded room, with a drumming demonstration going on in front of them, the woman nevertheless soon began to recover. Turning to Louise, she said, 'Well, I've done it!', to which Louise nodded and smiled. She had watched as the flame bathed her friend from head to foot.

Before looking at some more examples, let's recap because the message about the violet flame bears repeating. The seventh ray is the most powerful purifying agent in the cosmos, and because of its ability to clean up 'negativity' or low vibrational energy on a massive scale all lightworkers are to be encouraged to use it as often as they can.

As spirit and matter draw closer together (see Chapter 5) and begin to overlap and integrate, each time we invoke the violet flame we are also in effect receiving a mini-downloading of divine information (sometimes called 'the language of light' – see page 124) to help purify and rejuvenate yet deeper and deeper parts of ourselves.

To describe the phenomenon in physical terms, think of your own body or Mother Earth's as having infected wounds. The best sequence of events for a rapid recovery would be removal (= violet flame) of the harmful bacteria first, and then stimulation (= other cosmic rays) of the body's own curative know-how.

Where to use the violet flame

Here are a few more instances of where you might usefully invoke the violet flame, although there is no place, situation or being that will not benefit from its effect.

Try it out in a room where there has been an altercation or where people are still quarrelling. Paul, a young surfing enthusiast with a wise head on his shoulders, came home one day to find his father and partner Helen in a 'steaming argument'. After invoking the violet flame, he walked out and left them to it. Ten to fifteen minutes later, he returned. Helen was tenderly rubbing his father's feet, their anger having vanished into thin air. Paul was not at all surprised, as he often does a similar thing at his pool club where excitable players worse for wear from alcohol antagonise each other. A good sweep of the bar in his mind's eye with purple soon calms frayed nerves.

You can also use the violet flame for a general spring clean of your house. Jean explained how after she moved house she followed a little routine of her own in each of the rooms because there was an unpleasant odour. Afterwards all she could smell was lavender! Another lady, Marion, even invoked the flame in her home because she had lost a battery charger and badly needed to find it. As soon as she had finished, she felt compelled to pull out her bed, and there it was!

Have a go in car breakers' yards, tunnels, cities, restaurants, shops, hospitals, doctors' and dentists' surgeries, laundrettes, pubs, public toilets, shops, traffic jams... and around military establishments, landfills, accidents and sacred sites. The last suggestion might seem odd, but all sorts of people are drawn to such places for a variety of reasons and their energies are fed into them. The violet flame can help restore balance.

For situations or places that may benefit from the effects of continual transmutational energy, some people place suitably charged crystals at strategic points. A local woman, for instance, put amethysts in plant pots outside a nearby pub in order to purify the atmosphere each day in and around the building.

The power to change

If you reach a sticking point in your life or you would like a different outcome from the one that seems to be presenting itself, bring the violet flame to bear on the issue. If it is for the greatest good, you may be thrilled by a surprising result. A lady attending Louise's evening classes was able to verify this fact for herself.

Her son was in the process of buying a flat. All was proceeding well until at the last minute the vendor lost his job and had to withdraw from the contract. Her son was devastated. Not really believing it would have any effect, she nonetheless visualised the man surrounded by violet. The next morning, the phone rang for her son. It was the man to say an offer of a job had come totally unexpectedly out of the blue. The sale of the flat then went through perfectly smoothly.

Andy, a skilful craftsman when called upon, was making a dresser for a contact. He went down to a local skip hire centre to talk to the manager about obtaining old, recyclable wood. While he was engrossed in conversation, Louise seized her chance to move around the smelly piles of debris that littered the yard and invoke the violet flame. Andy was told to come back the following week when, hopefully, there would be something suitable for him.

To their amazement the very next day a huge skipful of wood was delivered right to their doorstep. Not only was their wait for this abundance cut to nothing, they did not have to collect it either – which spared them a great deal of strenuous physical effort. By using the violet flame, events at an energy level were moved along at impressive speed.

The power to heal

Healing can take place in many ways and by many means. If you are not a 'hands on' healer you can still make a difference by hugging, talking or listening to someone. Or, as in the case of surfing Paul as he is fondly known, you can send violet light to a stranger in distress and out of reach.

While on holiday in Morocco, Paul and a friend were sitting in a café when a dishevelled man stumbled in through the door. He was frenetically moving his jaw backwards and forwards, and the rest of his body was also in a general state of unrest. To help the poor man, Paul invoked the violet flame while his friend sent a blessing. Within 'five minutes at the most' there was a substantial improvement in his demeanour and he became much calmer, so much so that he was able to sit quietly at a table and eat the plate of food put in front of him.

If you're a complementary therapist, use the violet flame to prepare your work room and materials, such as crystals, before each session. Some therapists like to have a purple sheet or blanket on their couch and some even paint walls in the same colour. How about putting violet glass paint on light bulbs, too? Or wrapping the part of a client's body that may be injured in purple cloth? The ray's vibrational energy will be projected through the colour of any material.

Then use the violet flame again for yourself and your client before you start. This will make both of you more receptive to healing energies, as channels will become clear and you yourself will be working to optimum capacity. It's like removing boulders from a path – once out of the way, you can walk confidently and quickly along, unhindered by time-wasting obstacles.

If your therapy involves taking 'negative energy' away from a client, do remember to cover it in purple or ask for it to be transmuted. I mention this because Louise came across some therapists who would unceremoniously dump such energy at the end of their table without really considering what would happen to it.

After enjoying Louise's humorous images of people walking by on the street below being slapped in the face by a flying mass of nastiness, a lady admitted her husband was always in a foul mood whenever she gave treatments. It turned out that her healing room was upstairs in her house and that all the negativity she drained from her clients was being directed downstairs, to exactly where her husband was sitting watching television.

An immediate effect of the violet flame on a person's energy field can be detected in the aura – as already noted in Louise's second aura photograph on page 167. If you do not have easy access to an aura photographer, you might like to try the following with a friend or a willing client/patient to prove this fact for yourself. Using a dowsing rod or pendulum, ask to be shown how far the aura extends from your volunteer, including back, front and sides. Make a note of distance(s) and then invoke the violet flame. It does not matter who says the invocation, as long as it is for the person being dowsed. Take the measurements again, and notice the difference.

Louise and I have worked with sceptical groups of volunteers to test this exercise. In nearly every case there was a substantial increase in the size of the aura after the invocation – usually it more than doubled (it never receded), and any indentations and irregularities were smoothed out so that it assumed a uniform distance all the way round. (Imagine the effect your dynamic, violet-flamed aura could have on those you come into contact with during the day!)

Several people also said they were much calmer afterwards. This was a revelation for one of Louise's closest friends and mentor, Hazell, who before we began felt 'fragmented' due to unaccustomed pressures during the previous twenty-four hours. She was astounded at how her usual equilibrium was restored so quickly and so effectively. And with such little effort.

A couple of us even tried dowsing a small tree in the garden, with the same astonishing results – its aura grew by over two metres. This leads us to suggest that the violet ray could be usefully employed while gardening, especially if pruning or lopping off larger branches. It would sooth any distressed plants and pave the way for quick healing of damaged tissues.

The reason for the efficacy of the violet ray would seem to be that part of its function is to energise and balance all energy systems. Its effect can be felt on physical, mental, emotional and spiritual levels, and sometimes you will notice this for yourself straight away. A group of reflexologists were introduced to the concept of the violet flame at their regular monthly meeting and were requested during meditation to imagine the fire going to any part of their body which was troubling them. A woman had an annoying ear ache which had been bothering her for a while, so she concentrated on that. Within two minutes the pain had gone.

Other, more deeply seated problems may take longer to solve. One invocation on its own will not usually result in an instantaneous, longterm cure, but it will start the ball rolling. And the more the violet flame is used, the greater its cumulative effect. It will help you discover and work on the root of your difficulties, which is why, when combined with affirmations, it makes a powerful ally.

Think of those occasions when you do not know where to turn or how to deal with your challenge. It is as though you have a hallucination-inducing fever, and you need something cool and soothing that will break the high temperature before clarity can return. The violet ray knocks down those barriers which are preventing you from seeing your true path, and presents a window of opportunity for other rays to work their own special magic.

Louise and I invited reiki and spiritual healers, along with volunteer patients, to take part in a series of violet flame experiments. We asked the healers to spend about five to ten minutes giving healing in their usual way, and then to call upon the violet flame either for themselves and/or for their patients before a further five minutes of healing.

In the majority of cases there was a marked contrast before and after the invocation, with patients feeling a greater amount of energy and/or peacefulness, etc during the second segment. The healers were aware of sudden sensations in their hands, such as increased heat or coolness (although this was not necessarily felt physically in the same way by their patients), and Amanda, a young mum-to-be, said, 'After the violet flame there was an enormous surge of energy. The difference was as clear as between black and white... there was a ball of pins and needles energy in my hands.'

When Amanda was in turn given healing by Lucille, Lucille had a spectacularly life-enhancing experience. Her flushed face as she was telling us about it shone with excitement. She explained, 'I've only done reiki 1, so I wasn't sure about giving the healing, but everything was fine. For the first five minutes it was OK. Then, after the invocation, I didn't really need to put my hands on Amanda, because I felt as though our energies had already connected and merged. There was a wonderful feeling of oneness – to experience that was fantastic. I could actually sense molecules of energy linking. I didn't want to come back "downstairs". It was a real blessing.' Amanda caught some of the exhilaration too. She confessed it had been quite a shock when Lucille had put her hands on her shoulders; she described the moment as being 'almost unexpected'.

After I had invoked the violet flame for one of my volunteer patients, Mark, who was sitting in an upright chair with his eyes closed, a purple heart shape appeared for him within his third eye. He said it had not been there beforehand and that it stayed throughout the second healing period. He also described how his back became extremely painful and at one point he wondered whether it was the chair. But he realised it was not that at all (he had been carrying some very heavy business burdens of late) and the discomfort passed. He then felt absolutely fine.

On a separate occasion different healers and their patients had similarly exciting stories to relate. After the invocation Angela felt a rush of energy shortly before 'transcending' or 'leaving [her] body and going "upstairs"'. Vicky could see images in her mind at individual pixel level; the scenery then faded as though she could put her 'hands through into other dimensions'. Josephine also spoke of how she felt her hands would actually 'melt through Louise's body'. Most agreed on a 'more mature energy', one that could be both 'strong and steady' and yet 'soft' as well.

However it was verbalised, it seemed to fuse together bonds of love between people and to expand our understanding and experience of oneness – what Lucille had marvellously described earlier as 'molecular disintegration', a phrase she remembered being given to her many years ago while contemplating a carving of Jesus in York Minster. She recalled being moved to tears by the figure's exceptionally beautiful hands and, putting herself in a mother's shoes, asking 'What happened?' The words that came to her are perhaps a way of describing Jesus's own ascension...

For those people in our experiments who did not experience such dramatic differences before and after the invocation, it is assumed they were already more or less well balanced on all levels. One patient, Marion, just felt 'much brighter inside', so it is hardly surprising that Sue, her healer partner, did not really sense much, if any, change. As with many forms of healing, the body takes what it needs, however much or little that may be. It was also interesting to note that the one person among our groups whose aura did not enlarge had received acupuncture the day before, although she did go on to feel a shift in healing energies during the healing experiments.

I am most grateful to Liz for forwarding a note of what happened when she and a healer friend tried invoking the violet flame for themselves quietly at home, well away from a workshop situation.

This is what Liz wrote:

Giving a 10-minute healing session without invocation
I worked with a friend, who I consider to be a very strong healer. The energy around us both was pulsating and it felt very much like working in a magnetic energy field – very static and raw. My partner had had an extremely busy few days. The time for her to receive some healing was long overdue!

Receiving a 10-minute healing session without invocation
Again, this felt very static/electrical. My ear buzzed. I did feel very relaxed (this was also overdue for me!)

Giving healing after invocation
Everything felt much calmer. I felt a dome of energy (like a snowstorm ornament) engulf us both. There was a sensation of draining 'gunk' into the ground. (I believe my partner felt a sensation of things draining away.)

There was no need to do any hand positions with regard to balancing chakras. I am sure I saw Mother Mary.

Receiving healing after invocation
I felt static around my head. Saw to the right of me, at head level, a clear sphere with electricity in. I felt I was resisting the power, not willing to integrate it into myself. I felt very tearful and wanted to surrender.

Another healer, Jane, had a similar experience she was eager to share with us. She rounded her email off with the following upbeat statement: 'Since I have been invoking the violet flame I have been far more clear sighted in my healing and psychic fields and I feel I am a better worker for it.'

When Louise and I discussed the permutations that had been explored during our experiments and by healers subsequently, we agreed that an ideal healing or therapy session will comprise the following:

protection for healer + violet flame for clearing the room + violet flame for healer + violet flame for patient (ideally spoken by patient, but for those not yet receptive to the idea to be invoked by healer)

This alchemical formula can be adapted and used anywhere and for anything. It can even be employed for those souls who have passed over but who, for one reason or another, are unable to move on. On a couple of occasions Louise has been called upon to assist with clearing 'unwanted presences' from people's homes. The first was actually in a house at the back of her own.

While she went about her business, Andy stood by and watched. Never having come across violet in his own life, he felt somewhat helpless. And although he did not doubt the effectiveness of what his wife was doing, he still quietly thought to himself it would be nice to have some proof of its validity. In an instant, a flash of violet whizzed across the room, giving him the evidence he had requested. It was just enough to satisfy his curiosity.

The power to inspire

Designers, whether they know it or not, are gradually bringing the power of the violet ray into all areas of our third dimensional life. It can be quite entertaining, but also very revealing, to spend a few minutes analysing the benefits which the colour purple brings to familiar (and not so familiar) objects.

As a starter, how about underground pipes, latex gloves used by forensic scientists and clothing worn by hospital theatre staff? On a television documentary the other day I noticed with delight how members of an African tribe were all wearing matching deep violet t-shirts as they paddled their hand-crafted boat down river through dense jungle.

If you are seeking inspiration for yourself, perhaps with a project at work or a hobby at home, try invoking the violet flame before you start or before calling for assistance from the ascended realms. It will polish your receptors to creativity and open you up to endless possibilities. In conclusion, be inventive – use the violet flame whenever and wherever the mood takes you.

Enjoy the miracles, and let us know how you get on.

Meridian	Max	Max	Min	Min	Rise	Rise	Fall	Fall	State	State
Lymphatics	52	**57**	52	**57**	22	**30**	0	**0**	balanced	**stressed**
Lymphatics	62	**63**	59	**61**	60	**25**	20	**10**	stressed	**stressed**
Lungs	46	**48**	46	**48**	11	**27**	0	**0**	weakened	**balanced**
Large intestine	54	**62**	54	**62**	11	**24**	0	**0**	stressed	**stressed**
Nervous system	76	**57**	76	**57**	51	**15**	0	**0**	stressed	**stressed**
Circulation	50	**54**	50	**54**	12	**27**	0	**0**	balanced	**stressed**
Allergies	50	**48**	50	**48**	14	**32**	0	**0**	balanced	**balanced**
Cellular metabolism	44	**66**	44	**66**	20	**42**	0	**0**	weakened	**stressed**
Endocrine system	52	**63**	52	**62**	23	**35**	0	**0**	balanced	**stressed**
Endocrine system	56	**66**	56	**64**	27	**30**	0	**25**	stressed	**stressed**
Heart	50	**58**	50	**43**	15	**60**	0	**21**	balanced	**stressed**
Small intestine	49	**50**	49	**50**	38	**35**	0	**0**	balanced	**balanced**

Visible proof of the power of the violet flame! 'The BEST system' of computerised health screening, using acupuncture points, can detect imbalances in the body. With the help of Yvonne King of Meridian Health Screening, Andy was tested twice: once to assess 'base' readings (see figures in italics) and again, 2 minutes later, after a violet flame invocation (see figures in bold). You don't have to be a medical expert to detect noticeable changes in the second set of data. The violet flame immediately stirred up Andy's metabolism, bringing to the surface things to be healed

Violet flame meditation

This is a lovely meditation which leads you through the Garden of Peace to the Temple of the Violet Flame for purifying and healing. Use it on your own (tape the words beforehand if you can) or in a group whenever you need a pick-me-up.

Take yourself to a quiet place where you will not be disturbed and ideally wear loose, comfortable clothing. Sit with your feet firmly on the floor and have your hands on your knees or in your lap. Close your eyes.

Be aware of any sounds outside the room. Listen for a few moments to them and then bring your awareness into the room. If there are noises there, let go of them and any thoughts linked to them. Focus on the sound of your own breath. Is it shallow or deep? Then take a deep breath, hold it for a count of three and let it out. In your own time, repeat this three times.

Now that you are relaxed prepare yourself for the start of a journey. You are going to visit a new place, although when you get there feelings of familiarity may sweep over you. If this is the case, do not question or doubt your feelings – just go with their flow.

Your journey begins in a beautiful garden. It is a warm and sunny day, the grass is green and lush beneath your feet and the air is heavy with the perfume of many flowers. You walk slowly through the grass, noticing the scented blooms all around, their trumpet-like shapes swaying gently in the breeze. Everywhere you look there are brilliant colours, and yet it seems there is a pattern and order to the planting of the flowers.

Red flowerbeds soon give way to deep orange ones and these in turn change to sunshine yellow. Next you are not sure if you are walking through grass or flowers as there is a vast area of green all around you, but you can make out the same trumpet shapes. As you continue, their form becomes more definite and the colour changes to the clear blue of sea on a summer's day. Then the path carries on into an area of deep blue flowers which eventually fade into soft violet.

Just when you think you have experienced every possible colour, the path turns and you enter a new part of the garden.

Here is a riot of different fantastic colours – aquamarine, magenta, gold, peach and white. They almost dazzle you with the intensity of their light. And when you look more closely at the white flowers, they are more than pure white – they contain the essence of every colour in the universe.

This is surely a very special place as it radiates such love and warmth. You may feel you want to stay in this beautiful garden for a while.

Eventually your gaze falls upon a building at the edge of the garden between some tall trees, and you start to walk towards it. It is large, circular, very solid looking and white. There are huge pillars at the front and there is a domed roof on top.

You enter the building and immediately become aware of the energy within. It is giving you a feeling of joy and there is a hum in the background. You then notice that all round the inside of the building there are huge quartz crystals. Behind them, the walls are smooth, white and like marble, and the floor is a deep amethyst colour. There is great power within this place, yet it is softened by peace and love.

You are just beginning to adjust to the feel of the room when you notice a large silver circle in the centre of the floor. It is directly beneath the central point of an amethyst cluster in the domed roof. You are intrigued and you find yourself walking towards it.

Without hesitation you step onto the circle. At once you become aware of a change as the whole room turns the most perfect violet colour. The quartz crystals sparkle and reflect the violet light, and as you look about you you then realise that this light is at its most intense around you.

You look down at your feet and they are standing in a column or shaft of the same violet light, which links the silver circle and the amethyst domed roof. And as you look more closely, you realise that it contains a range of shades encompassing all hues from purple to violet.

You then become aware of a gentle heat which seems to permeate every cell of your body. It starts in your feet and then it slowly spreads to your ankles, calves, knees, thighs, into your base chakra area, your abdomen, your solar plexus, your heart, throat, third eye and crown. Your whole body is warm and tingling as if you are under a shower and there is a great feeling of release followed by calm. Just as a shower cleans and washes away, you are letting go of worries and fears. You may be aware of a change in your mood or state of being. If there was tension or unease in your body before, you may find that this has diminished. You now feel lighter, even less solid. Take a few moments to soak up and enjoy this feeling.

You have now been cleansed and purified by the violet flame and you step off the circle. As you do so the column of violet light decreases in intensity until it finally fades away. You find yourself walking towards the door of the building, and as you leave you take one last look at the magnificent room with its quartz and amethyst crystals.

You then retrace your steps through the garden with its vibrantly colourful flowers – white, peach, gold, magenta, aquamarine, violet, deep blue, sea blue, green, yellow, orange and red. You are now at the place from which you started.

Bring your awareness back into your body and listen to your breathing for a few moments. Slowly move your hands and feet and, when you are ready, open your eyes.

CHAPTER 5

New energies and new chakras

Once you are on your ascension path, there really is no going back unless, of course, you make an uncharacteristic decision to veer off down some wayward track. It's an unlikely scenario: even though every second of each day presents you with choices between light and dark, your regular spiritual practices will be attuning you with your higher self, and the more focused you will be – wild horses will not drag you away from your heart's and soul's desire.

Making this strong connection with your higher self, and maintaining it whenever possible, is an important element of mastery. Although technically it is not quite the same, some people talk about it in terms of realigning themselves with their 'Christ consciousness' or allowing their Christ consciousness to unfold. Basically what this means is opening up to the unconditional love within you. Regular use of the violet flame will help enormously in drawing to the surface any hindrances that may be preventing you from being the loving, forgiving person you really are.

Keys in the past

You have probably already come to an understanding of how crucial it is to forgive yourself as well as other people. It is certainly true that until we have dealt with even the tiniest scrap of guilt, and eliminated the word from our vocabulary, we will probably keep feeling frustrated with ourselves and we might not even realise why.

Sometimes, however, guilt, forgiveness and other major anxieties that are impinging on our lives in a manner we cannot necessarily detect easily can stem from an unexpected source – our past lives. If this is to be your last incarnation, buried past life blockages must be cleared on physical, mental, emotional and etheric levels so that you can be fully cleansed. There may also be aspects of yourself which have become fragmented or scattered along your various paths in different incarnations. You now need to reassemble and assimilate them into your whole being.

When you are ready to handle issues, they will be brought to the fore for you to deal with. This can be as simple as acknowledging whatever strikes a chord with you. You might not comprehend the whys and wherefores of what has gone before, but that does not matter.

The timing must be right for you, and it is not always possible to force the pace. I remember spending a miserable weekend on a past life/regression course, listening after each meditation with increasing dismay to what seemed like fantastic feedback from everybody else. They talked about meeting their guides, walking round ancient cities, wearing sandals in a desert, passing over in magnificent temples… All I could say in embarrassment was 'I got absolutely nothing!'

I can laugh about it now, but at the time I felt a complete failure. What I did not understand was that this was not the appropriate occasion for anything to be revealed to me. I had gone with suspect intentions – with little comprehension of reincarnation, guides or spiritual laws, I saw it as a bit of a lark, like another scalp to be added to my collection of paranormal experiences. And perhaps I needed a gentler introduction than could be given in only two days.

Since then a number of past life echoes have reverberated for me during my sleep. I will give just one example here. Several years ago I went through a phase which lasted about twelve months of dreaming week in week out about boats, rivers and seas, and people being pulled out of water, half-dead and needing resuscitation.

Checking the symbols in dream dictionaries, I assumed my emotions were being let off the lead at night. The colours black and white featured over and over again too, in a multitude of guises – from black and white people to black scripts on white backgrounds.

The last image I had on this theme was of a grave, rather like a sarcophagus, on a boat which was under water. Being interested in archaeology, I wondered in the dream whether it could be excavated (in hindsight, rather an appropriate analogy). The next morning I soon forgot about it and drove over to my friend Sheila for one of our regular healing sessions. After she had finished, I asked her whether she had received any visual impressions – she had previously confided that from time to time she would see pictures in her mind's eye that were relevant for her patients.

'Yes, I did,' she replied, much to my surprise, 'There was a rocky cove, rather like the coast around here, and a large sailing boat was lying on its side in the sea.' 'Was it a modern boat?' I enquired. 'Oh no,' Sheila said, 'It was a very old one... it was black and white!' She did not elaborate much more, but said 'It must have been very unpleasant for you, as I think you probably died in this incident...'

All the dreams I had had over the last year, especially the one from the previous night, seemed to punch me in my stomach. You can imagine my reaction. From that moment onwards I have never had any more dreams about boats, water, drownings or black and white. It has also made me wonder whether as a very young child my intense fear of water and swimming was due to some hang-over from this particular lifetime. Whatever it was, and I am not terribly interested in discovering the fine details, it has gone from my subconscious mind – one less dead weight to be carrying along my spiritual path.

As a fascinating aside, when I was about twelve years old my family were holidaying in Norfolk on yachts. These beautiful craft, 8 metres or so in length, were built in the 1930s and '40s from mahogany and, according to the yard from which we frequently hired them, were uncapsizable.

One morning my mother and I were with a couple of novice sailors, happily coasting along in a stiff breeze. Within minutes the wind blew up to almost gale proportions, and a freak gust blasted down the river. We never quite worked out exactly what happened next, but we suspect a short piece of thin rope used to tie up the sails at the end of the day managed to become wedged in a block on the boom. This meant the rope attached to the sail could not run freely. Instead of letting go of it, which would normally happen through sheer force of excessive wind on sail, one of the novices was somehow able to cling on, and over we went into the murky water.

I don't recall anything after that, but apparently while my mother was trying to grab hold of her friends, one of whom could not swim and the other had a heart condition, I instinctively climbed up onto the keel and rocked the boat until it eventually righted itself. I had never had any lessons, so how at the age of twelve did I know what to do? Was karma from a past life event being balanced in some way? It is curious that no other boat in the fleet before or since our mishap – that's 60 or 70 years plus – has ever capsized.

Louise has learned about some of her past lives very differently. One of her experiences started as a teenager when she went on a school trip to Provence, to what is commonly referred to as 'Cathar country'. While they were there the weather was beautiful and warm, and they spent much of the time out of doors in swimming costumes. After a few days she developed burns on her lower legs, but nowhere else, and she was in a great deal of pain. This was surprising, given that shoulders and backs are usually the most vulnerable parts of the body.

Louise's teacher insisted she just had sunburn, but Louise was never very convinced by this explanation. She did not think much more about it until a couple of years ago when in the February she had trouble with her legs again. They itched and burned, and were generally most uncomfortable. Louise invoked the violet flame to bring relief to her symptoms, and a flash of inspiration came to her.

The Cathars were a Christian sect who flourished in the south-east of France during the 12th and 13th centuries. They believed in great purity and that most of the material world was evil. Many were burned at the stake for their supposedly heretical views. Perhaps she, too, had been burned in this way and this was why her body's memory cells were reacting so violently: the injustice of the act as well as the intense pain and terror associated with flames licking her feet and legs (most people would lose consciousness or be dead before the fire reached much further up the body) could no longer be held within her energy systems and had to be expunged.

As these thoughts were running through her head, everything seemed to click into place. The catalyst had been her visit to Provence which her soul had intended she should experience to bring the deeply rooted fear into her consciousness – as a young girl she could not have ignored the physical signs, though at that stage she was not yet fully equipped to resolve matters.

Now she knew with certainty that she had been put to death as a Cathar. She could even remember the staked chains locked round her ankles getting hotter and hotter in the flames, and realised that the very places on her legs which were currently giving her the most irritation were where these chains must have been. Needless to say, with some more concerted violet flame work her legs recovered and that past is well and truly behind her.

The reason for talking about past lives here is that ascension requires us to master our chakras. Anything which continually adversely affects our mind, body or emotions must be addressed at some point. You can see from the two examples I have given that however hard Louise and I were trying to remain balanced on all levels, intangible forces were hijacking our longterm prospects. Until we had recognised the signs and investigated the causes of our troubles, it would have been impossible for us to be eternally at peace with ourselves.

So before moving on to consider the exciting prospect of new fifth dimensional energies entering your chakra system and creating substantial changes within it, check in with yourself to see whether there are any unresolved affairs in your own life that might relate to previous incarnations. Look for clues in your dreams, extreme likes and dislikes, messages you receive every day from the universe…

And don't forget your friends and family. There are at least three women living nearby each of whom has one child who is confused about what happened to their 'other mummy' who they can describe in intimate detail. 'You're not the mummy I had last time' seems to be the children's common remark.

Ask your higher self and the ascended realms for insights and for easy ways to achieve resolution. Your progress to enlightenment will not stop if the past is still haunting you. In fact, if you are open to possibilities and you face them when the opportunities arise at the right moments for you, you will already be demonstrating multi-dimensional mastery.

Reflections on the past

If you wish to be more proactive in exploring some of your incarnations, a consultation with a skilled hypnotherapist can be a good *entrée*. Some people discover that through hypnotherapy and regression their longterm ailments disappear completely in a short period of time or even on the journey home.

On the other hand if you do not fancy that idea, but your curiosity has been aroused and you would like to do something in your own surroundings, try the following. It can help you connect quickly with the energies of who you were in one or more of your previous lives. Results are not guaranteed, but when things do happen they can be startling.

Stand in front of a wall mirror or, if you do not have one at a comfortable height, a hand-held mirror is fine. Breathe deeply two or three times and relax your shoulders. If you have not already surrounded yourself with protection, now would be a reasonable moment to do so. Ask your Godself and the ascended masters to help you see whatever is for your highest good at this time. You might also invoke the violet flame, as this will clear your spiritual vision and still your mind.

Look at your face and then let your eyes go slightly out of focus, as though you're gazing through your reflection (it's the same technique as when finding the 3-D image in magic eye pictures – see opposite). What do you see? Are there any changes in your features? Is there anyone else standing with you?

You might not see anything, which is fine – it might not be an appropriate time for you to be exploring or maybe you have already dealt with your past life gremlins. If you do notice something, ask yourself why. Information gleaned in this way can be helpful in shedding light on the qualities you have brought with

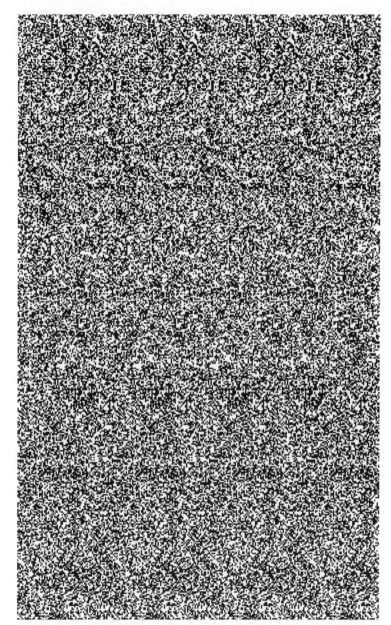

'Magic eye' – hold the page normal reading distance away and let your eyes go out of focus so that you are conscious of the whole pattern area, not just one part. Give yourself time and wait for the image to appear

you into your current life and the lessons you need to learn.

The first time I tried this exercise on my own I was shocked by a stern-looking woman returning my stare. With her hair scraped back from her austere face into a bun, she reminded me of a frightening governess. There wasn't a flicker of joy or fun in her face, and I immediately thought about my tendency towards seriousness. With that sour image in front of me, I vowed to uncover the more playful aspects of myself for a better balance to my personality.

Louise used this exercise with a group of friends in Hazell's house. Most people were holding mirrors in their hands, but Cathy, a lady interested in shamanism, did not have one so she went out of the room and stood in front of the hall mirror.

After about quarter of an hour, when the others were deep in animated conversation, Cathy came back in and sat down, announcing that she had 'done it' and it had worked, but she had not liked what she had seen. She became rather distressed, and when asked to share her experience she described a face whose dark eyes were 'evil'. She felt as though this was herself in a past life in which she had committed some gruesome crime.

If you find yourself in a similar situation, your natural reaction will be to feel shock but don't panic! Most of us will have killed, murdered, tortured or perpetrated some other horrific crime in at least one of our lifetimes in order to learn what is right, and what it feels like to walk in darkness rather than in the light.

Breathe deeply and invoke the violet flame. What is being reflected back to you may simply be a sign for you to acknowledge those parts of yourself which you would rather not admit to in this lifetime.

Be honest with yourself. Are you compartmentalising your spirituality? Like many people, I used to bring mine out of its box when I mixed with like-minded friends or when I meditated, and put it away again when I considered myself behaving in an 'unspiritual' way. Gradually it dawned on me that we are all divine beings all the time, and that those aspects of ourselves we might not particularly like are nevertheless still a precious component. It can be rather comforting to realise that absolutely everybody has them, and they can provide some of our most valuable lessons.

Other people at Hazell's had somewhat pleasanter stories to tell. Gladys watched as her face almost disappeared, then 'went rubbery' and she felt that an oriental man was with her. Ken's eyes faded and he wondered whether he had been blind in a previous life. Sue could see a long white moustache on her face, while Hazell noticed a flower, like a daisy, appear in one of her eyes, where it stayed until she put the mirror down. The flower raised an interesting point for discussion, as the motif can represent the 'flower of life'. This is an alternative expression for our light body, a subject I will come back to in Chapter 6.

Mandala members several months later also reported similar findings when they spent an interesting evening experimenting with mirrors. Gerry witnessed an astonishing array of characters fleetingly superimpose themselves on his face – a docker, a vicar (he was aware of the dog-collar), a Mongol, and an Egyptian (the painted eyes were clearly visible). Jo watched as her reflection aged into the head of a man whose features were much broader than hers, and Cheryl noted that the image shown to her in her mirror had much darker hair and bluer eyes than hers. There was much for people to ponder on.

Hazell subsequently gave us even more to think about when she described how on another occasion one of her friends thought the figure in the mirror was the one observing her. Unnerving as it must have been, it may have encouraged her to clarify her views on past lives and what exactly she was tapping into.

As further food for thought here, could it be that many of our guides, such as those perceived by clairvoyants, are actually aspects of our higher wisdom which are represented as images of ourselves from different incarnations? This is a fascinating concept which seems to make sense if we consider how our souls are directing us to achieve our own mastery. It is so true that the answers to our problems can usually be found within us rather than from external sources.

The mirror exercise can be taken a stage further, and can even be treated as an entertaining game to play with close friends or family. All you need do is divide people up into pairs. Then, if they can manage to refrain from laughing, they should spend five or ten minutes sitting in front of each other, looking at each other's face. The feedback can be intriguing, especially if they have already used a mirror on themselves and can match up their own experience with their partner's.

The Mandala group were again willing guinea pigs. This time when Gerry sat with his wife he saw her face morph into that of an old man with bushy eyebrows and a 'malevolent, murderous' expression. When Cheryl looked at Hilda, Hilda's left eye became smaller and her face grew thinner. From a side-on perspective her countenance was that of an elderly man, described by Cheryl as a sea captain who had a white beard and wore small round glasses.

My partner Marian, who is one of the most intuitive people I know, did not notice any visual changes when she held the mirror to her own face. However, through tuning into her inner feelings she had a marked sense of ageing, which tallied with what I had seen.

This was another important reminder: if you are using a mirror on your own, and you are not able to make out any visible changes (sometimes they are subtle and easy to miss), take a second to tap into how you are feeling in yourself and in your body. Are there any alien emotions or unfamiliar aches and pains? The mirror is just a tool for accessing the past, and whispers from it may be replayed for you in whatever way is appropriate for you at that moment – which may be something unexpected in order to attract your attention.

Acknowledge anything out of the ordinary, no matter how small or seemingly irrelevant, and ask forgiveness of those you may have harmed in a previous life as well as giving yourself a forgiving hug. You might also like to finish with one final invocation of the violet flame to sweep away the last few cobwebs.

Being able to talk through experiences with a sympathetic partner can obviously be helpful and may be all that is needed to release energies from previous incarnations that are still hanging over you. When Louise was working with a woman called Mandy, her attention was drawn to the fact that only images of young people and children passed over Mandy's face, and she sensed a great feeling of sadness.

When they chatted about it afterwards they were both aware that, although Mandy is in her 30s and has children of her own, she has retained a child-like quality to her voice. She admitted she has clung on to this from being a small girl, and has also been unable to shake off a fear of vomiting. They deliberated over whether these clues pointed to several lifetimes in which Mandy never reached full adulthood.

What happens now?

It is no mean feat being ever vigilant over thoughts, words and deeds, so give yourself some credit for what you are doing and what you have achieved so far. You have probably already taken it upon yourself to develop a wide range of spiritual tasks and daily routines, and to learn to go with the cosmic flow, doing only what inspires you from the heart.

In addition you may be contemplating working more diligently with the rays and their colours and/or reaching out to the ascended masters as part of your spiritual expansion. You deserve a round of applause for your endeavours – congratulate yourself on your progress, and do the same for anybody else you know who is bravely treading their path of truth.

Your friends in the higher dimensions are also honouring your efforts. As you continue to raise your vibration, they will draw even closer to your ever strengthening light. At the same time spiritual wonders will begin to manifest themselves in and around you. These emblems of your mastery, the last few gifts you need to guarantee your ascension, will give you greater access to divine knowledge as you walk your road of enlightenment.

The phenomena I shall describe here and in the next chapter run alongside one another. They will occur in response to your increased spiritual awareness, understanding and commitment, and are like cogs in a huge set of wheels that are intricately linked and finely balanced.

As you attract to yourself greater influxes of light, they are set in perfect motion. The processes are overseen by the ascended masters, the angelic realms and friends in other dimensions in conjunction with your soul which knows when you are ready for them to happen, so there is nothing to be concerned about. They are a mark of your progress.

Discovering remarkable truths

Many people fully embracing their spiritual path are unaware that momentous events are occurring within and around them. Others, however, find that acclimatisation to new, powerful energies produces out of the ordinary physical sensations and/or unusual thoughts and emotions.

This is where being able to exchange views with like-minded friends can be so comforting but also very uplifting. It took Louise and me a year or more to figure out exactly what was going on, and during that time our excitement mounted as we gradually realised the import of what was being revealed to us.

If you're not sure about the manifestations in your own life and you don't have any one to confide in or bounce ideas off, set aside a quiet time to listen to your heart and intuition. Look for signs around you. Ask for confirmation or clarification from your higher self and the ascended masters and angels. Most of all, don't worry. Everything is in perfect divine order.

When Louise first mooted the idea at workshops of new energies affecting our physical bodies via our chakras, there was a sense of awe and of relief too as more and more people revealed their own experiences. Therapists from different parts of the country confirmed that, although they did not know why, they had recently been increasingly drawn to work with clients' legs. Many of the non-therapists could understand the reason. One lady had convinced herself that the aches and pains in her knees which had been niggling her for some weeks were because she had been standing for too long. Others complained of having 'too much energy', particularly in their feet, and, unable to keep still, of the need to walk and stamp about, sometimes in the middle of the night.

Alternating bouts of heat and cold featured among the list of 'symptoms' as well. I was what you might call fortunate, since mine happened while I was asleep. In dreams I was aware that my hands were freezing cold even though the bedroom when I woke up was quite warm. Louise on the other hand did not have this luxury: she felt every twinge and swing in body temperature very keenly during her often extended waking hours.

The night before a violet flame course, for instance, she sat huddled on the end of a settee. She had just spent nearly a week 'burning up' with what seemed like a fever (but it was not a real illness), and now it was as though she had ice crystallising in her blood. I could even detect the frostiness in her aura. She pulled her clothes tightly around her, and promptly went to lie on the floor in an attempt to work through whatever spiritual energy was affecting her.

After a few minutes she suddenly sat bolt upright and blurted out rather mysteriously, 'I've seen him again!' No one knew what she meant, so of course we asked her to clarify her statement. She explained that several weeks earlier the image of a man wearing a sort of trilby hat, glasses and a long coat had come into her mind. And just then this same picture had again sprung out of nowhere while she was resting on the floor.

We laughed as we spent the next ten minutes guessing who it might be. Was it Saint Germain playing a joke? Unable to reach any sensible conclusions, we let the matter go, and were glad to hear from Louise that she now felt fine.

Out of those present Andy understandably looked the most relieved. This was not the first time his wife had given him cause for concern over the previous twelve months. He would often wake up in the morning to a pair of feet on the pillow next to him! Unable to rationalise her feelings but willing to follow her instincts, Louise kept changing her position in bed to cope with the energy fluctuations she was going through and to achieve the rest she was finding so elusive. It brought success every time.

Fretful, aching knees, legs and feet... a man in a trilby hat... strange sensations and sleeping patterns... This seemed to be a bizarre collection of experiences, but Louise and I were convinced they were in some way connected to new fifth dimensional energies. In the end we were right: they turned out to be fantastic clues to higher spiritual knowledge. But before all the remaining pieces could be set into our wonderful mosaic, there was further work for us to do.

Several months after the man-in-the-mac episode, Louise had channelled enough key words, symbols and phrases, including 'star tetrahedron', and had received sufficient guidance through dreams and so on, to establish a working theory about the changes to the chakras. When she talked me through it I confess I was unsure about her leaps of faith, as my limited understanding had come about through the use of crystals.

A friend had given me a set of 'chakra balancing stones' for a birthday present, and I eventually got round to trying them out. To my delight I discovered that without looking at them I could tell which was which simply by holding a crystal in my hand and noting the part of my body which reacted to it.

This was great fun until my root chakra seemed to travel downwards. One evening as I was clutching a red jasper I felt a definite sensation in my thighs. A week later it was in my knees, and the next occasion brought a very unsettling feeling in my shins which led to uncontrollable jerking of my legs. When I tried other crystals my bewilderment increased, because nothing was behaving as it should. What on earth was going on? It was as though everything had been thrown up in the air and had not yet settled back into place. Enough was enough. It was time to put Louise's theory to the test.

We invited three perceptive and accomplished healers, Josephine, Vicky and Angie, to take part in another experiment. We asked them to scan Louise, surfing Paul and myself for chakras or strong energy centres, and we made it clear that they should remain open to the unexpected, that they should not necessarily assume chakras to be in the conventional positions, although it was quite possible they might be.

With these scant instructions they each took it in turns to tune in to us. They were in different rooms so they could not confer with one another, and they jotted down notes on cartoon sketches of our bodies. Needless to say the drawings by our amateur artists prompted gales of laughter, but the net result of their efforts was astounding: they detected similar features in all three of us, some of which contradicted usual chakra positions and energy signatures.

They admitted they had been puzzled by what they were sensing, but had followed our limited brief to the letter and had put doubts to one side.

Their findings, which I will bring in later for comparison when talking about the implications of the new chakra arrangement (see pages 99-108), seemed to confirm that Paul, Louise and I were all more or less in the same phase of a dramatic chain of spiritually driven events.

Before moving on, a few symbols seen and sensed by two of the healers are worth mentioning here, since they also helped verify Louise's hunches. When Angie was working with Paul she first of all felt a spinning energy around his head.

As she moved her hands further down his body, everything 'seemed normal' until she reached his knees. At this point she sensed and drew on her diagram a 'V' going up to his shoulders and onwards and outwards, which she later described as 'like an upside down rainbow in that the colours were reversed'.

Vicky saw in her mind's eye a butterfly around Louise's solar plexus area and a hand to the right of her face, which actually tied in with one of Angie's remarks about Louise, that 'there was a pull to the right side of her body'. I will return to these findings shortly to reveal their meaning.

So, after the experiments, the theorising and the tying together of every tiny piece of information, here is the explanation of what we had been investigating and deliberating over for so long.

Spirit and matter uniting

Once you have cleared and more or less balanced your chakras by spring cleaning every nook and cranny of your life (you may not always maintain perfect balance, but you won't ever be far out), your soul recognises this achievement by metaphorically opening the door through which you can draw to yourself from the fifth dimension a new set of higher spiritual energies.

This is in accordance with the spiritual law of attraction which decrees that like attracts like – it is as though you become a powerful magnet pulling to you only the most precious of metals.

The set comprises five divine essences whose vibrations resonate to the fifth dimensional colours and qualities of the five
new celestial rays, namely clarity (aquamarine), balance and harmony (magenta), eternal peace (gold), divine purpose and joy
(peach), and transformation (opalescence).

Over an indeterminate period of time (length will depend on
your body's rhythms and how quickly you adjust, and is likely to
take months rather than a few days) the essences will ultimately
be combined with your chakras. A helpful comparison can be
made with upgrading a computer.

By improving the software and perhaps modifying the com-
ponents, you can substantially enhance a computer's memory,
speed and overall efficiency. It will look the same on the outside,
but its internal overhaul will allow it to perform much better
than before. In a similar way your body's own hardware, its
chakras, can be boosted by assimilating high vibrational spiritual energy – the equivalent of downloading updated software.

As soon as the amazing conversion has happened, you will
then be equipped with what Louise imaginatively calls a master
power pack. This will maximise your ability to love unconditionally and to take on and radiate more light. Having access to
fifth dimensional attributes within your very core will also
enable you to fulfil your mission effectively – one of the most
important responsibilities you have is to play your part in assisting Mother Earth to activate her own light body (this will be a
major theme in the next chapter).

To explain the 'light expansion process' – the integration of
the five sacred chakra energies – I will rely on two geometric
shapes which have deep metaphysical symbolism: an upward-
pointing triangle, representing the physical body or matter (in
sacred geometry it is associated with the known universe), and
some distance above it a downward-pointing triangle, representing spirit or spiritual energy.

For our purposes the process is set in motion on the soul's
signal when the upper triangle begins to move down towards the
lower one. It meets it (remember Paul's 'V' rising up from his
knees? draw a line across the top of it and what do you have?)
and then overlaps and locks to form a *tetrahedron* or a star with

six points, also known as the Star of David. Some view the inter-locking triangles as symbolising wisdom and harmony, but they can also be interpreted more broadly as encompassing every aspect of our spiritual path. They demonstrate that we really are creating for ourselves bliss on earth.

Continuing with the triangle analogy, figure (a) on page 162 shows matter divided into seven segments to represent what are widely accepted as our major chakras – seven vortices of energy over specific parts of our physical body. Spirit has five segments – the five spiritual energies descending from the fifth dimension. Imagine the leading point of the upper triangle piercing each of the seven chakras in turn as it moves down, starting with the crown and working downwards to the root, and infusing them with divine qualities.

There is an obvious parallel here with the kundalini, another form of spiritual energy, though perhaps less refined, which moves in the opposite direction. It spirals upwards and pene-trates the chakras from the root to the crown as reawakening to The Source is kindled. The light expansion process is a reverse of the kundalini and is an acknowledgement of full awakening which brings with it true self-empowerment.

While the two triangles or contrasting forces are coming together – you might envisage them in three-dimensional terms as pyramids – their collective or macro energies spin in opposite directions to each other: one spins clockwise and the other anti-clockwise.

This might account for the disorientation, lightheadedness, twitchiness or sense of not being grounded that some people experience at this stage. Then, when the transformation opales-cent micro energy is over the heart centre, movement of the tri-angles stops. The large contra-spinning energies merge into a single mass which orbits the body in one direction, a state which can be maintained for a while.

Next come even more amazing events. To compensate for the fact that the fifth dimensional essences have entered and are being integrated, minor or secondary chakras we already have in our feet, knees and hands are upgraded to take on the function of primary centres. Finally, at a moment again determined by the soul, the orbiting energy shoots outwards in all directions to the outermost parts of our energy grid (the grid will be discussed in the next chapter) and then stabilises.

Before it reaches equilibrium the locked triangles or pyramids rotate by 180° and the chakra energies move to the positions shown in the diagram on page 107. When the body has adjusted to these modifications, the light expansion process is complete. And that – as far as Louise and I currently understand it and in the most simplistic of terms – is that!

You may have to read through this section several times in order to understand the whole procedure. If you do, you may no doubt appreciate the difficulty Louise and I had getting our heads round it all. Having drawn the two triangles on a piece of card, with chakras written on both sides, cut them out and placed them over each other, the analytical genius in our team found it especially difficult to make sense of what happens after they interlock. Nothing made spiritual logic. How did the chakra energies reach their ultimate locations?

However hard Louise manipulated the cards, she could not fathom the conundrum. We agreed yet again that working with the ascended masters is certainly never dull – although we might have to put in a great deal of effort, it wouldn't be half the fun if everything was handed to us on a plate...

One night as she was tossing and turning, she was reminded of those countless occasions when she felt compelled to sleep the wrong way round. The message which had been thrust at her time and time again suddenly became crystal clear. What she had been doing was altering her position by 180° or *reversing*. She wondered if this was the answer. Even though it was only five o'clock in the morning, she leapt out of bed and grabbed the two cards. She then did as the word impressed on her mind suggested – she 'flipped' them. The problem was solved in an instant.

The next morning her endeavours were rewarded with an angel card which trumpeted 'Victory'. She later heard of other people's reversal experiences – one person had been through an above average number of situations requiring her to drive her car backwards while another acquaintance rather strangely had to reverse the code digits on her combination lock to open it.

To summarise, think back once more to Paul and the upside down rainbow with reversed colours: does the beautiful image not encapsulate all that has been described? And one further thought on this astonishing sequence of events: the turning point is also a significant indication that we have fulfilled our solar destinies by reaching our final outgoing destination. We can begin to head back on the in-breath of God towards the Almighty as light-bearing – enlightened – beings.

The upgraded chakra system

So far I have talked in general terms about the divine essences merging with you, and of integrated energies moving to special positions in what has become a hugely augmented chakra system. The implications for you are wide ranging, because you are being taken to another level of your spiritual development. Your vast potential is becoming a reality, your possibilities for absorbing and radiating light are infinite. And the consequences of that are immeasurable not only for you, but for every other being on the planet and, crucially, for Mother Earth herself.

The reorganised chakras retain, or in some cases take on, third dimensional qualities associated with positions in the former system. But because they are now also infused with fifth dimensional vitality they operate at an elevated frequency and reverberate with profound spiritual wisdom. Should you suffer from dis-ease in the future, therefore, you may need to analyse the cause(s) of your imbalance from a much higher spiritual perspective than you might be accustomed to doing.

Here, then, is a list of the new chakras, with some of our healers' abbreviated comments in italics for interest before each description – remember the healers knew nothing about the light expansion process or its effects when they took part in the experiment.

Since seven energies from the old system and five from the fifth dimension added together apparently make twelve, I will talk in terms of twelve new chakras – see the diagram on page 107. The chakras at feet, knees and hands are counted as three rather than six.

Feet (7)

'there were hot spots at the ankles'... 'before the heels'... 'on the tops of the feet... and maybe underneath the feet but I couldn't reach under there!'

The upgraded chakras in both feet contain the energy from the old system's crown chakra, our original connection to The Source and to oneness. With the injection of high vibrational spiritual energy we have the opportunity to advertise our link with the divine by truly 'walking our talk'. No more sitting on the fence: our choice is made, so we can shine brightly with love and joy in that secure knowledge.

That is not to say you should go out and evangelise indiscriminately – not everyone wants to or is ready to hear your truth – merely that you should try to seize opportunities presented and trust your intuition to tell you what to say and how to act in any situation. You may never utter one spiritual word, but the way you conduct yourself will be a dazzling advertisement. Have the confidence – you are a master.

As the chakras are balls of energy around the feet, people will feel and pick up on them in different ways – perhaps some will find hot spots on the tops and around the ankles, and some on the soles, just as our healers did.

If you ever have problems with your feet, it might be worth considering whether you are hiding your light under a bushel! In Hazell's case, however, it was just a question of not being aware of the transformation she was going through. She told Louise she must have been doing too much decorating because her ankles were giving her a lot of trouble. As soon as she heard Louise's explanation, the pain literally disappeared instantaneously and has not returned since. Her body knew something unusual was going on, and it needed only the lightest of reassurances from her conscious mind to relieve its anxiety.

Knees (6)

'definitely hot spots on the knees'... 'just above the knee joint'... 'backs of the knees'

The combination of new essences and old system third eye energy, which urged us to look intuitively within to see who we truly are, now encourages us to declare our divinity through humility, devotion and service to others. It's rather like going down on our knees, humbly showing we are the same as the next person and willing to celebrate the fact. In the case of Dr Rowan Williams, freshly appointed Archbishop of Canterbury, that is precisely what he did when he reinstated the Maundy Thursday tradition of bathing strangers' feet. For decades it was omitted from the job description of this most senior of Anglican posts, but by bringing it back Dr Williams demonstrated publicly his commitment to helping others, whatever their needs might be.

As with the feet, there is a chakra in both knees. This really echoes the balance we seek between the two sides of our body, between our masculine and feminine aspects. Through our own strength, tempered by love and compassion, we can empower rather than overpower those we wish to nurture.

Hands (5)

'the hands felt hot'… 'the palms of the hands were pulsating'… 'hot spots at the elbows… tops of the shoulders…forearms'

The old system fifth chakra was concerned with communication and taking care over what we thought and spoke. The new spiritual blueprint expands on these issues and deals with communication in its widest sense. Consider how heart warming it is to see someone offering you outstretched arms – the affectionate gesture is the personification of love, of the divine spark in us all.

Whenever you hug someone, hands, arms, elbows and shoulders all play a part in surpassing spoken words, so it is not surprising the healers registered patches of energy extending from the hands upwards. (I have confirmed to my own satisfaction that during healing sessions energy really does emanate from my forearms.)

You may find yourself touching or hugging much more than you used to do, even gently placing a hand behind a person as you open a door for them or wait for them to pass. Go with your instincts, for Love is never embarrassed.

Base of the spine (4)

'the root seemed to be where I would expect it, sort of tilted underneath'... *'hot spot around the coccyx'*... *'and on the tops of the hips – not what you would think'*

The old fourth chakra or heart centre was often called the bridge between the lower and higher chakras. It was the meeting point between earthly and spiritual matters, and when in balance enabled people to love unconditionally. In the new system its essence is linked with that of the root chakra, to security and 'fight or flight' issues.

With the fifth dimensional energies also added to the equation, the resulting blend provides you with the means with which to act and react from your heart at all times. In other words, instead of feeling fear and on occasion being paralysed by it, your life can be governed constantly by love.

When it boils down to it there are only three alternatives we ever have to decide between: we can go with fear, with our ego's desires, or with love. When we hand ourselves over to the Will of God, the last of these will usually be our first choice and in time it will become the only one because the others will have disappeared through lack of selection.

The chakra is most obviously felt at the base of the spine but it also extends in a band right round the hips and lower abdomen (front and back).

I've already briefly mentioned reviewing health issues from a higher spiritual perspective. On a basic level the light expansion process does not affect the endocrine glands. They are still linked to the chakras in the torso and head. However, for many people who are going through the process or who have already done so, the conventional links between blockages or imbalances in specific chakras and specific ailments may no longer hold true. Healers and therapists in this field may need, without passing judgement, to intuit what stage patients and clients have reached if traditional methods for pinpointing sources of problems are not working. Here is another example to help you build up a picture of how you can help yourself and others by being aware of new possibilities.

A man with lower back problems, who has been on his spiritual path for some time, goes to a therapist. The therapist starts by simply asking him if he hurt his back recently, perhaps by gardening a little too enthusiastically. The answer is no. Then she tries to probe a little deeper to discover whether physical difficulties, such as losing his job or not having enough money to pay the bills, are creating symptoms. The responses to her second set of questions do not bear any fruit either, so, recognising the man is interested in spiritual issues, she then proceeds gently to a different level and enquires about love and fear in his life – has he maybe resorted to meeting his challenges the hard way by letting his hang ups take hold?

By talking through his problems in a calm and loving environment, the man reveals that his anger is getting the better of him. He has recently allowed it to rule his relationship with his wife, because he has become fearful she may leave him for someone else. Although he has no grounds on which to suspect his partner, his irrational, fearful self has misinterpreted genuinely innocent behaviour. Once he has voiced his concerns and addressed his fears head on, his back heals.

Mid to lower abdomen (2 and 1)

'the general mid to lower abdomen area was very different from what I expected; the spleen chakra was above the belly button, not where it usually is at all'… 'it was like a line of chakras which made my hand shake up and down'… 'there was a sensation of a football spinning between her body and my hand'

It is no wonder the healers were confused by what was going on in this area of the body, because there is a bunching together if not in some people an amalgamation of two chakras to fit the space! Their combined energy signature is very powerful.

The old system root and sacral energies permeated with Source attributes effectively mean that as we hand ourselves over completely to God we are to create with wisdom according to divine will.

I recall a few days when it seemed that whenever I glanced down at my body, there was a brief flare of pale blue in front of my midriff. My thought processes went from blue to the first celestial ray to divine will to a meditation on the very subject that week at Mandala. But in hindsight I suspect it was a sign to confirm what I am describing here. The positioning of the colour right over my body was so precise.

Talking of colour, it was interesting to note that the healers were not particularly aware of our chakras' hues, even Vicky who said she was usually 'very hot on colours' – she saw a few, but not many and there was no consistency between them. Perhaps this was fortunate, as we might have become sidetracked by trying to analyse the ramifications of each person's colour codes. With the light expansion process we are obviously in such new territory that there is naturally much still to be revealed and documented. There are many questions yet to be answered, although we can make some informed guesses.

My own view of the new chakra system is that its colours depend on an individual's distinctive vibration. Having practised karate for a number of years, I will take an analogy from the martial arts to illustrate my point.

Traditionally, every martial arts student learns from a master who, through years of conscientious study and practice, demonstrates perfection of movement and technique – although a master never stops learning and practising. Theoretically, if you could put masters from different centuries together in the same room there would be no difference in their performance – the purity of their art would have been transmitted perfectly from one generation to the next.

But of course that would not be strictly true. The reason is that once students eventually become so adept as to reach the status of master, sometimes marked by a change to the belt worn during training (in the West coloured tags or script are often added), they can then, and only then, subtly allow their own individuality to be expressed through their art.

Now that we are mastering the third dimension we are each being given a unique combination of energies in acknowledgement of our proficiency. These match our needs and personalities, and the way they are expressed through colour will therefore vary from person to person.

Solar plexus area (3 and 12)

'I got a throbbing in my palm over the solar plexus'

The old system solar plexus chakra was a centre for transforming the self into a powerful being at one with the world. So it is no coincidence that the fifth dimensional transformation energy is now also within the solar plexus centre, a fact confirmed by Vicky who saw a butterfly, symbol of transformation, over this area of Louise's body. We are being offered much additional help to maintain balance while leading an active life, because in a nutshell if we are ill or tired we cannot go out and walk our talk.

Heart (11)

'there was a throbbing, strong heart chakra'... 'it was as though the solar plexus and heart chakras had joined into one big oval: they couldn't be separated'

How often are we exhorted to undertake only what makes our heart sing? With divine purpose and joy in our hearts, we can focus more closely on consistently making the daily choices that will allow it to do just that. If your head is telling you you ought to do something, you may be led to a decision requested by your personality or ego. Double check your motives. Do they give you a melting sensation inside? The more open and loving you become, the larger your heart chakra will be (as detected by the healer here), and the more you will feel fulfilled in all you do.

Throat (10)

'there was a marked energy at the back of the neck at the joining of the skull'... 'I was confused over the whole throat chakra section, as there was something around the mouth area too'

Some of the healers' perplexity during our experiment may have been due to the size of the chakras – they were perhaps larger than might have been assumed. The light expansion process literally increases the amount of light and energy held in all parts of the body's systems, and particularly in the chakras. The strong refined vibrations extend well beyond the confines of the old centres.

Eternal peace is the divine attribute held within the new throat chakra. For most people well down their spiritual path gossip is a thing of the past anyway, but now communication becomes more than just being careful in what we say. We should actively speak peace by allowing the love in our hearts to be heard through our voice and words. For those preparing to channel verbally, it is especially important that the throat chakra is kept clear and pure; more experienced channellers may regularly find a marked accumulation of energy around their throat, mouth and back of the neck.

Third eye (9)

'the third eye was absolutely open – like a Cyclops!'... 'it was right across and including the eyes'

Balance and harmony are the keys to this chakra. It's like having in your head the sort of tool (aptly named a 'spirit level'!) which carpenters and builders use to make sure surfaces are flat. Look carefully at everything you are given in life to ensure the bubbles – your choices – are in alignment with your soul's guidance.

Louise had been preparing for some considerable time to leave her school career so she could devote herself wholly to spiritual teaching. But the opportunity that would allow her to do this as well as meet family and financial responsibilities had not yet arisen.

One day she thought the answer to her prayers had dropped into her lap. The staff at her school were informed that the jobs of two teachers had to be lost in an attempt to curb rising expenditure. Voluntary redundancies were being sought from any department. Louise spent a week deliberating over whether she should put herself forward for what in monetary terms could be a beneficial package. Was this the chance to follow her dream and do what makes her heart sing?

Each day she thought and thought about the possible future an immediate release from school duties would bring her. But every day an unpleasant throbbing in her third eye could not be ignored. She sat down to analyse her situation: in spiritual terms was she in danger of losing balance or had she lost it altogether?

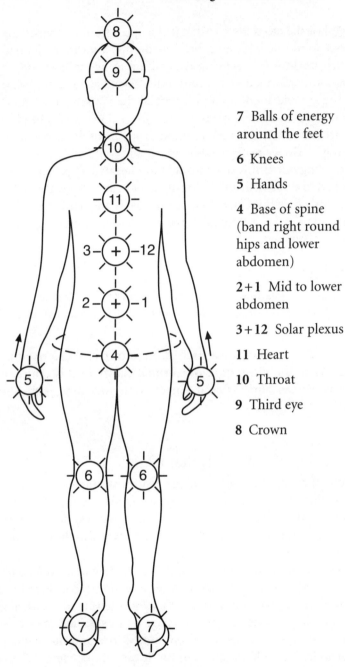

7 Balls of energy around the feet

6 Knees

5 Hands

4 Base of spine (band right round hips and lower abdomen)

2+1 Mid to lower abdomen

3+12 Solar plexus

11 Heart

10 Throat

9 Third eye

8 Crown

Positions of the new chakra energies

At last she faced the fact that if she opted for redundancy the school would be without a head of drama, a position she had battled for in order to bring recognition to her subject and its capacity to affect students profoundly. Take that away and what message would it convey to the rest of the school community? She could already hear them saying 'Oh we don't need a head of department... Drama isn't an important part of the curriculum anyway... Do we really need drama at all?'

Bowing out at this stage would have negated all past actions. She had to stand firm and hold true to her convictions about her students' education. Her decision, probably the hardest she has ever had to make, was finally arrived at. And the pulsating in her third eye stopped.

Crown (8)

> *'the crown chakra was fully open, with energy like a narrow shaft of light coming into the body and all the way down to and through the feet'*

As a result of working on ourselves, our crown chakra is opening wide. With the integration of spiritual clarity in this centre, it means we can aim for clear, direct communication with The Source at all times.

Is that it?

These, then, are the twelve energy centres through which flows the divine life force. Before our experiment we thought that that would be the end of the story. But Vicky noted two further energies above our crown, one roughly 25 cm away and the other two thirds of a metre.

Louise and I pondered on these, bemused by what we initially felt should not really be there. After a while we concluded the most likely explanation was that Vicky was sensing the closeness of our Christ consciousness. On page 81 I explained the Christ consciousness in terms of unconditional love and our willingness to let it unfold in our lives. But it can also be viewed as the mediator between our physical self and our soul.

As we evolve spiritually and become masters in our own right, there is less and less need for information to flow via an intermediary – our vibrations are such that we can establish a direct connection with our Godself. Not wishing to lose a valuable asset, however, we can allow our Christ consciousness to merge with us in the third dimension. This is another part of our ascension, and must take place before we can unite with our I AM presence.

After Louise and I had warmed to the idea, we forgot about it and several weeks passed. Then Louise happened to pick up a book in which it was stated that the Christ consciousness is often represented by the symbol of a hand. She had not come across this before, and neither had the rest of us. Nevertheless what had Vicky also seen around Louise that day? A hand to the right of her face! Yet again, splendid confirmation after the event.

The final confirmation

If, like me, you have a mind which often throws out sceptical thoughts (there is nothing wrong with being a walking question mark!), you may still be wondering whether the light expansion process is an impossibility, the result of overactive brains. If you are, the following may raise one or both eyebrows at least as far as your hair line.

It all started innocently enough when Louise bought a book for Andy's birthday. He has a passion for reading and is always hunting for titles about ancient Egypt, the Knights Templar and so on, usually subjects Louise does not feel drawn to explore in any great depth. Her main interests lie elsewhere but are complementary to Andy's, so they invariably find themselves reaching similar conclusions via different routes.

Louise had managed to get hold of a brand new publication, *Lost Secrets of the Sacred Ark* by Sir Laurence Gardner, that was right up Andy's street, and she was determined he should not be allowed to look at it before his birthday. She was about to hide it away from his clutches when something made her stop and open it. Before she knew it, she was engrossed in the text. She did not even hear Andy enter the room. After a bit of leg-pulling, he made her agree that he could take his present to a talk the author was giving in the area in a few days' time. An autograph would naturally be a birthday bonus.

Louise had been assuming the evening would be a case of wife accompanying husband to keep husband company. But after snatching a brief glimpse at *Lost Secrets* she was having doubts about that and was wondering whether information gleaned would actually have an important bearing on our interpretation of the light expansion process.

As they sat in the audience waiting for things to start, Louise looked towards the platform and was utterly flabbergasted to see the man in the hat, glasses and long coat who had popped into her mind weeks ago at Hazell's.

After the formal introductions she was even more amazed to learn that it was Sir Laurence himself. She dug Andy in the ribs, turned to him, eyes wide with excitement, and whispered something to the effect that this was going to be a very interesting night.

That, indeed, was what it turned out to be. Sir Laurence Gardner is a distinguished researcher who began his career investigating the aristocracy of Europe. He is also recognised in scientific circles and has since risen to prominence as an advocate for the so-called platinum group of metals.

Although they are extraterrestrial in origin, these platinum metals have been found in huge deposits on earth – presumably the result of meteorite impacts. Their potential for revolutionising the world is enormous: applied in the right way they could be used for curing disease; providing cheap, sustainable and clean energy; facilitating time travel and making other science fiction fantasies a reality – warp speed, matter cloning, teleportation, etc, etc are within reach.

I won't attempt to summarise all of Laurence Gardner's work, mainly because I could never do it justice, but I will offer a very condensed version of what is most relevant to this chapter.

In scientific fields it is becoming increasingly evident that what was previously impossible will become possible because of what happens to the metals when they are heated to very high temperatures. It has also been discovered, or more accurately rediscovered, that gold reacts in the same way – hieroglyphics on tombs and elsewhere suggest ancient cultures, including the Egyptians, Mesopotamians, Babylonians and Alexandrians, acquired and used this knowledge to benefit their kings and pharaohs.

When solid gold is heated beyond 1000 degrees centigrade there is a sudden great flash of white light before it turns to what looks like talcum powder. The platinum metals are also transformed into powders which are known to scientists as 'orbitally rearranged monatomic elements' or 'ORMS'. Sir Laurence and others are now calling them 'the most magical substances in the universe'; some people prefer the less poetic but equally descriptive 'exotic matter'.

Heat transmutes gold into what is classed technically as a superconductor. Superconductors have incredible properties, the most fascinating of which for our purposes is their ability to 'attract, hold and pass on energy without dissipation'.

In other words they can keep absorbing energy to produce more and more light – as Sir Laurence says, 'there is no limit to how much light you can keep piling into a space'. They also communicate via light frequencies. If you continue to heat them, they disappear completely from sight, and then when they start to cool they reappear.

During experiments scientists suspected the powders had merely become invisible to the naked eye, but when they attempted to mix them with other substances they soon realised that this was not the case at all. They must actually have been in another dimension!

The Egyptians called transformed gold 'MFKTZ' (pronounced 'muffkutz') and saw it as a key part of their leaders' enlightenment. They believed that each person has a light body which needs feeding in the same way as the physical body does. It seems from pyramid symbols that MFKTZ, a food of light, was their most valuable commodity and that they mixed it with frankincense to make bread cakes. These were then eaten by the pharaohs to promote a long and active life unblighted by disease.

But could MFKTZ really enhance physical health as well as give spiritual sustenance just as the Egyptians believed? Well, it has now been demonstrated that when an atom of, say, ruthenium is placed on the edge of a short strand of DNA it in effect shouts 'Boo!' at the DNA and causes it to go into shock.

The result of this is that the DNA becomes one thousand times more conductive; the helix literally falls apart and when the atom of ruthenium is removed it rebuilds itself according to its original code. The implications of these early experiments for the treatment of such illnesses as cancer are huge. If mutated DNA can be made to revert to its proper coding, no more tumours...

Other superconductors have been shown to produce similar phenomena – put simply, they sneak up behind atoms, the atoms become scared, forget who they are and go into a high *orbital spin*; they then *reverse* and go off, *transformed*, in a different direction...

By now you may be detecting uncanny parallels between the mechanics of what happens when platinum group metals are heated and when electrifying spiritual energy kickstarts the light expansion process – although in our case we are not so much shocked as given the opportunity to make physical adjustments in our own time.

I also like to compare our pure divine state with gold. We may have gathered a few so-called impurities along the way during our various incarnations (which the violet flame and our own spiritual work can deal with), but the heart of our being is unblemished. And like transmuted gold, we become superconductors able to absorb ever increasing quantities of light whose brilliance illumines those we meet and helps activate our own and Mother Earth's light bodies.

The finale

As a footnote to Louise's story, a couple of days later she started to listen to a cassette which she and Andy had bought at the talk. It was a recording of one of Sir Laurence Gardner's presentations earlier in the year.

She was stunned to hear him described thus: 'This is the man who is known as the Count St Germain of the scientific world.' She jabbed at the off button on her machine and sat in silence.

You could have heard a proverbial pin drop while she thought about the implication of that statement.

I think it is quite simple. Louise, representing proof via 'spirit', and Sir Laurence, representing proof via 'matter', are brought together by the ascended masters, principally St Germain, to reveal the entire light expansion/transmutation picture. It may still be a little fuzzy, but the complete composition is there for all to see.

As above, so below. As below, so above.

CHAPTER 6

The merkabah and the light body

Modelling a starship

Louise and I were never very good at geometry at school, so when we were mulling over what a six-pointed, spirit/matter star might look like in the third dimension it is hardly surprising that all we could do was stare blankly at each other and giggle. But then Louise's practicality kicked in and she went off in search of what every self-respecting teacher has in her visual aids bag – a bunch of pipe cleaners.

With much help from number two son, who muttered under his breath something to the effect that women's spatial awareness is somewhat lacking, they assembled a series of interconnecting triangles. The finished product, much to our surprise but not to Matthew's, was an eight-pointed figure.

When we stood back to admire their handiwork, we laughed at the pretty pink and purple, albeit rather spindly, model. Here was matter and spirit fully integrated on the kitchen table! And then we smiled again, because here also was a fuzzy little merkabah.

Like the upgraded chakra system, our merkabah (a word taken from Ancient Egyptian) is an end product of the light expansion process. Some people describe it as two counter-rotating fields of energy – after the two triangles or pyramids of spirit and matter have locked into position around us and rotated through 180°, they then start spinning in opposite directions again.

However you view it, your own merkabah or star of light offers you tremendous scope to handle new, exciting opportunities with confidence. Once it is up and running and placed, as it were, in neutral gear, you will begin to feel your spirituality in every fibre of your being. Your 'off' days will become fewer and fewer, you may experience a more heightened consciousness, and forgiveness and boundless compassion will become your favourite mantras. That is not to say you will no longer be presented with lessons, but you will be better able to face them head on and you will invariably wish to contemplate them all from an elevated spiritual perspective.

During an autumn workshop Louise was constantly bombarded with difficult questions from one lady in particular. This in itself was not a problem – tough probing can be a gift, testing how far we are prepared to walk our talk and at the same time leading to all sorts of revelations. But as the day wore on it became quite clear that this person was following her own agenda.

Late in the afternoon Louise's patience was pushed to the limit by yet another barbed comment. Instead of snapping at the bait, she merely acknowledged her own mastery and repeated to herself several times over: 'I AM a Master. I rise above this'.

As she did so the boundaries between dimensions blurred: the walls seemed to dematerialise and in their place were fifth dimensional colours, notably aquamarine and magenta. The woman too was surrounded by the luminescent colours. After a few moments, clarity and balance tangibly reached the physical room and Louise, who managed to retain her equilibrium despite the spectacular experience, continued the conversation seamlessly, the walls now having returned to their conventional solidity.

In hindsight Louise wondered whether for what seemed like a few seconds, but was probably only a fraction of this, she travelled into another realm. As a spiritual superconductor, had she achieved this feat by raising her vibration to such an extent through positive intent and increased light absorption that it 'activated' her merkabah – put it into first gear?

It has been said that our merkabah is like our own special vehicle for travelling across time, space and dimensions, and there is certainly anecdotal evidence of people spontaneously disappearing on one side of the world and reappearing on the other. (The talk several years ago of alien space craft visiting the planet and taking off those ready to ascend might have come from a misunderstanding of the true nature of the merkabah.)

You do not have to be consciously aware of yours for it to become a new integral part of you. You might, as spirit and matter have now integrated, see flashes of third and fifth dimensional tones around you from time to time or catch sight of larger portions of your kaleidoscopic starship – colours and their combination will depend on your unique essence. Or you might feel an invigorating energy. But if you don't, rest assured that whenever there is cause for your merkabah to be activated, perhaps during especially difficult challenges when physical and spiritual senses need to be boosted, it will happen for you automatically, quite naturally and probably without you knowing about it.

As has been said before, spirituality is about simplicity and allowing yourself to advance at your own pace. If speed really is important to you and you want to rev up your merkabah quickly (you might question yourself why you feel this way), you don't have to follow complex procedures – the most potent driving force of all is complete unconditional love. It's the best fuel in the universe.

When you are in tune with yourself you will feel your heart centre grow as it develops into an ever flowing spring of this unconditional love. It will become a very real component of your body – roughly mid-way between your solar plexus and your neck. The next time you act in a selfless manner, note whether you feel anything in this area. Recognising which, if any, part of you is affected by the events of each day can be a guide to how balanced and loving you are. Your body will always tell you when ego or fear are taking the lead.

Some people have already progressed to the point at which, technically, they could put their merkabahs into top gear and move on to their next level of spiritual evolution. However, it is not uncommon for such individuals to be offered a choice between making that journey now or delaying it for a while. Ashian, for whom the ascended masters regularly manifest themselves in person and who teaches channelling, was suddenly overcome with excruciating pain. She collapsed on the floor and it took her five hours to crawl just a few metres to the telephone.

As she lapsed into unconsciousness she heard a voice telling her she had fulfilled her mission and asking her whether she would like to pass over. She thought rapidly about this and decided there was still much she wanted to do. She determined no, she was not ready to die. The next thing she knew, she was in hospital recovering from a life-threatening ectopic pregnancy. Ashian had generously chosen to continue in service in the third dimension.

Like Ashian, many of us will be around here for a little while longer and will make use of our merkabahs while keeping our feet firmly on the ground. And here I come to the crux of what ascension is all about. Mastery is certainly achievable this life-time and will, when the time is right, lead to an end of reincar-nation and to an enthusiastic welcome by our friends in the higher realms. But until that happens (I leave the precise date to those who like to speculate about such matters) we can also live our enlightenment, our own ascension, here and now on the earthly plane.

This might seem a contradiction in terms, but by letting go of fear and transmuting the denser aspects of ourselves we are brought back into the full glorious light of our true being. As co-creators with The Source through unconditional love, we can express the celestial perfection we experienced before descend-ing into the third dimension. No wonder the ascended masters are leaping up and down with joy at our progress – we are per-forming master miracles of our own making while still inhabit-ing, to use a rather antiquated phrase, corporeal vessels: our raised vibrations are indeed literally bringing heaven to earth.

More geometry

While Louise was receiving and analysing information about the light expansion process, I was sent off down another route. The adventure probably started with what I took to be a spiritual downloading. I had just returned home after medical treatment and was resting on my bed.

I catnapped for maybe ten minutes, and as I came to I was aware of a huge, perfect geometric figure in the middle of my inner vision. I could not fail to be impressed by its presence because running round its rim was a broad band of brilliant, fifth dimensional aquamarine. The colour was so gorgeous it naturally drew my attention, but after I had admired it for a while I managed to count the number of sides to the shape. There were six.

My next encounter with the same figure came about a year later. Again, prior to waking when my consciousness was alert but fluid and open to spiritual input, a plain hexagon outlined in black appeared. This time there was no additional colour. A few weeks later the image comprised a line of joined hexagons. As the months went by the line became several linked together and in turn a whole sheet, forming what I described to Louise as a latticework. Then proceeded the following variations on a theme – words in italics are key motifs I will come back to shortly.

In one instance the *hexagons* were outlined in *violet* (transmutational energy) *and gold* (transformed energy/light). In another the latticework was much more complex, with the sun (The Great Central Sun) *shining through it*. The view then shifted to a microscopic cellular level at which *symbols were flowing through capillaries*. This linked in with just one dream in which the latticework was formed from *diamond* shapes, and within each diamond was part of a symbol. The longer I concentrated, the more it seemed the symbols had been broken into pieces and *were being fed through the grid a segment at a time* (downloading). A further dream brought the hexagons back, this time with the silhouette of a crab in each one, and a fabulous calm, *blue sea*.

Gradually the grid became three dimensional and its outer framework viewed from a distance was that of a sphere. It was made from a multiplicity of geometric shapes but with hexagons dominating, and I could summon parts of it at will during brief lucid dreams. The *pièce de resistance*, however, happened when my eyes were wide open. It was about five o'clock in the morning and the telephone rang. I woke with a start, my heart beating fast at the disruption.

I looked across the bedroom towards the door, and all down the wall to the right of the door about three metres away was a lattice of golden hexagons. I blinked to make sure I was not hal-lucinating, but it was still there, glowing in the darkness. Its inspirational effect on me eased the pressures of the forthcom-ing day – the phone call concerned my elderly mother-in-law who had fallen at home and was in distress, having been unable to move for several hours from her painful position on the floor. Medical assistance, additional personal care, etc all had to be organised at speed.

And then the dreams of lattices stopped. For a while they were replaced by nightly scenes of wild flowers, but they too dwindled. By this stage it had at last dawned on me that a story board had been carefully constructed for me. The question was, could it be interpreted correctly?

I scanned my book shelves and was drawn to a title about crystals. I had bought it months previously but had not yet got round to reading it. I turned to the introduction, skimmed through the first few pages and then was stunned when I came across a drawing of one of my sheets of hexagons.

The text explained how atoms and molecules are organised into seven types of geometric pattern or *lattice*, including hexag-onal and orthorhombic or *diamond* systems, to form different types of crystal. (Interestingly, aquamarine has a hexagonal structure and some rhombic minerals can also form hexagonal crystals.)

I went on to read how the author, Michael Gienger, had made an intriguing discovery about people's gem preferences. He believes our character traits can make us predisposed to choose crystals with the same structure. I was not entirely convinced by his argument which made a correlation between crystals and life styles. Nevertheless out of curiosity I turned to the section in the book on the hexagonal lifestyle and in a matter of a few minutes read what amounted to an uncannily accurate appraisal of me, warts and all. I was fascinated by the fact that I had been made to look at the real me, light and dark, by just following a shape.

Was this what the dreams were intended to point out? Perhaps partly, for when I was telling Louise about my findings she was reminded of her near death experience dream in which the people at the end of the tunnel were not in customary human form – they were geometric shapes. However, we could not help feel there was more of the story to tell.

I flicked through my notes from some of Louise's workshops and came across a comment Gladys had offered after one of the exercises. She mentioned that during meditation she became aware of honeycomb cells within her body. That same day when Louise was travelling home she closed her eyes to rest and she too saw the image of a honeycomb, a layer of six-sided geometric figures.

Intrigued by this, Louise suggested she should ask the science teacher at school whether such types of cell have a part to play in biology. I agreed. His response was that proteins and connective tissue are, surprise, surprise, comprised of hexagonal cells, although under the microscope they might look slightly more elongated than a conventional bees' honeycomb matrix.

So, how significant was this piece of information?

Reviewing the situation

We considered all the data gathered so far. First of all there were the dream pictures, from lines of hexagonal (and diamond) cells, some containing symbols, to a complete 3-D framework of interconnected geometric shapes, mostly hexagons. Then there was the hexagonal (and diamond) structure associated with a certain type of crystal. And now we had building blocks within the human body to add to the equation. It had also not escaped our notice that the Star of David symbol representing the conclusion of the light expansion process has six points, and if you draw a connecting line between each of them you get a hexagon...

After ruminating for a while, I jotted down a few headings to summarise our detective work – 'Physical body', 'Crystal' and 'Spiritual'. Louise, who is very knowledgeable on the subject, then sparked the next bout of lateral thinking by mentioning Atlantis.

I have always found the concept of Atlantis difficult to handle, although I have never been able to explain satisfactorily why for years I had nightmares of tidal waves, miles high, looming in the distance. Just sitting through programmes about tsunamis made me writhe inside – I was terrified but irresistibly drawn to them by a strange, compelling magnetism. Then one evening as I was watching a huge wave the size of a skyscraper rolling towards me on television, it slowly dawned on me that my churning fear was no longer there.

When I look back, the vanishing act seemed to coincide with a demonstration of 'biogenesis' healing tools. The technology for these was apparently used in Atlantean days and has only recently been brought through by the ascended masters for people, in true master fashion, to help heal themselves. I offered myself as a volunteer for Sue, the person giving the talk on this eventful evening.

Sue wafted various instruments around my body and homed in on my solar plexus area where she said she detected a hole in my aura. She asked me whether there was something I needed to let go of, but I did not really understand what she was alluding to and was very conscious of the people sitting round about. So when she invited me to do it there and then, I declined and said I would work on the issue (whatever that was) later on my own. Louise interjected immediately and politely, but firmly, intimated we should carry on.

Louise later explained to me why she had spoken up in this way. Apparently spiritual energy had begun to swirl around me, which she strongly suspected was there for a definite purpose. A few minutes later, after Sue had called on the Karmic Board to release, if appropriate, past karma, she saw what she took to be an Atlantean face followed by a series of 'ordinary', predominantly male, faces (perhaps images of past life incarnations) superimpose themselves over mine. Then a large violet flame whirled by my left side while Archangel Michael stood as Protector behind me.

When I returned home it was as though I had received surgery to my solar plexus and I had to spend at least ten minutes giving myself healing to overcome the discomfort. Louise meanwhile had the same dream several times that night in which the message was: 'It was effective.' When we discussed this the next day we took it to mean the evening had gone according to a higher plan and that we did not need to know the details, although we suspected a very shady Atlantean past had been purged.

I digress, but I have included this episode to explain why I took Louise's prompting about Atlantis seriously. I decided the crabs, symbols of water, and blue sea could well tie in with this ancient civilisation where it is believed the physical make-up many of us assumed then was of a silicon, i.e. crystalline, type. And it is to a silicon-based form mankind is supposedly returning. Intrigued further by such speculation, I turned to the internet for some scientific grounding.

The first website I clicked onto took the wind straight out of my sails. At the top of the opening page about silicon crystal in bold type was 'Structure: *diamond*', and immediately beneath was a large, bold blue diagram of the atoms in a molecule of silicon. Looking at it from a two-dimensional perspective, if you drew a line between the atoms they formed a hexagon, and when considered from a third-dimensional viewpoint they made a cube or a figure with eight points. Hadn't we come across these before – in the explanation of the light expansion process and the merkabah? The next page on the website illustrated the structure of silicon in its solid state. To my untrained eye it was a series of hexagons joined together...

Having digested these facts I then wondered whether Louise's hints about human DNA currently going through a process of change also had a ring of truth to them. It is thought that abilities such as telepathy and clairvoyance were originally coded on the Atlantean 12-strand DNA, and were shut down when the Atlanteans abused their gifts – as a consequence their DNA was reduced to a double helix. Perhaps it is possible after all that the 12 strands are now being rebuilt at a time when those who are part of the ascension movement can prove spiritual knowledge will not be misused again.

At this point have a look at surfing Paul's drawing on page 168. Paul allows colourful, dynamic images to flow through his consciousness and he then transfers them onto paper – he often does not understand their meaning until after a picture is completed. In this instance, as he sat back to consider his work, he felt there was some connection with the make-up of the body at a cellular level. He counted the strands and found with astonishment that there were twelve. Could they, too, represent our Atlantean past?

A recent experience of Louise's gives a further slant on these ideas. She was sitting in her special secret garden at home, quietly enjoying the sun and the peaceful surroundings. Then she became aware of a blue energy nearby. She turned to her right and for some reason glanced at her hair. Incredibly, she could see each shaft at a microscopic level.

Most of the strands were composed from the new fifth dimensional colours but there were a few in conventional rainbow colours. We wonder whether she, like Paul, was being given evidence that the DNA and cellular changes taking place in our bodies will ultimately lead to the creation of a new fifth dimensional form. In which case we thought the three headings of 'Physical body', 'Crystal' and 'Spiritual' made a very apt and logical sequence.

Another part of the story

The tale has not yet reached its conclusion, for the latticework has a few more secrets to reveal. It can also be likened to a part of our aura, a golden light-packed layer which is much closer to our soul level than other layers. As we cleanse ourselves of lower vibrational energy and greatly increase our capacity to hold light, we start tapping directly into divine consciousness.

This pure awareness or infinite knowledge can be visualised as a golden grid of light which surrounds and connects every being on earth, including Gaia herself. The more we work on ourselves and use the violet flame, the more we wipe away films of dust from our own grid or 'light body' so that it illuminates us and everybody we meet.

By now you will no doubt be getting the hang of the violet flame and probably don't need much further prompting, if any, to try invoking it for yourself. But I would like to relate just one more of Louise's experiences which demonstrates more than any other where it can all eventually lead.

Louise was playing around with some new mirror exercises, and decided she would invoke the seventh ray. She expected to see violet transmutational energy in the reflection of her face, but instead she was somewhat shocked when golden light, like a halo, shone around her head. She guessed the image was to show complete transformation of lower vibrational energy into light, the culminating effect of the alchemical flame.

Transformation can and is being accomplished today. And as far as Gaia is concerned, her own detritus can be brought more quickly to the surface to be cleared if we work for her with the violet flame. Never underestimate your part in her ascension: you are as essential to it as water is to life. If you accept your responsibility and carry it out with a cheerful heart, you will share in the delights of her immense achievement as well.

Having a clean, sparkling grid also makes it easier for us to access the divine wisdom of the universe, including our own akashic records stored in our light body and those of humanity and the planet. Our soul, assisted by ascended masters and angels, will from time to time download us at strategic growth points with the so-called 'language of light' or spiritual information.

The knowledge we receive from The Great Central Sun via our light body helps us on our learning spiral and moves us further along our spiritual path. Interestingly, reiki initiations are a form of downloading, and the desire by increasing numbers of souls to make huge progress this lifetime may be why there has been an explosion of interest in this method of healing in recent years.

Downloaded information is often seen in dreams or spiritually as our old friends the geometric symbols – sacred geometry holds the essence of creation, including each individual's own remarkable make-up and their vibration (as perhaps represented by predominating shapes in their merkabah). You don't necessarily need to know what all the symbols mean. Trust your soul's guidance and enjoy the benefits. In addition, knowledge can be downloaded as colour, each ray emanating from Mother/Father God and containing different aspects of Her/His omniscience that we can assimilate easily.

And now we do at last come to the end of the story board, to dreams of wild fuschias and violets and to Hazell's daisy in her mirror exercise (see page 89). These pretty images of the 'flowers of life' are just another way of portraying the light body. They symbolise the single source of natural beauty from which we have all come and express our blossoming radiance, inter-con-nectedness, our oneness.

This loving support of one another encompasses Mother Earth too of course. As more and more people successfully uncover their light bodies and/or build missing parts, the greater the amount of light and information to which she also has access. This in turn will help her uncover the whole of her own light body. Once we have established this vast web between us she, like the spider in the middle, will be ready to leave the third dimension. And when she does, we will be invited to accompany her.

One last thought here. From all that has been said it seems that *Light*, equated with God/The Source/The Great Central Sun or whatever phrase you wish to use, has a number of facets to its make-up. Within its broad definition must be included spiritual energy, our life force, all knowledge, unconditional love and uni-versal symbols of creation (and in numerology, incidentally, the letters in 'light' add up to master number 11!) So the next time it pops into your conversation, or you are about to write it down, you might pause to consider the awesome magnificence of this small but powerful word.

In summary

Although this is the conclusion of our story, the spiritual narra-tive continues. In brief, many people already have active merk-abahs and light bodies, and are now in the process of fully inte-grating within themselves another very dynamic energy I have already mentioned on page 109, their Christ consciousness.

During several trips to London Louise learned much about its potential to impact on others, sometimes quite noticeably, although at first she did not understand what was going on. She was aware of a build-up of spiritual energy beforehand and assumed it was in preparation for her work. Then throughout her courses she was surprised by how many people gravitated towards her and stood just centimetres away from her for long periods of time.

A friend jokingly drew parallels with biblical scenes described in the New Testament, but she may have been much closer to the truth than she realised. Were folk subconsciously being attracted to Louise's emanating Christ Self vibration and enjoying its loving embrace? It's a strong possibility.

After integrating the Christ Consciousness the next piece of the action will centre around each of us merging with our I AM presence. This is a tantalising prospect I will touch upon again in Chapter 8. In the meantime here is a taster of what you can look forward to. Lucille was attending a residential course on colour and light, and towards the latter part of the week everyone was asked to describe what they had seen during one particular section. They were reluctant to voice their opinions, so the course tutor persuaded a courageous lady to go out to the front and give her feedback.

As she was speaking, Lucille could make out a golden figure close behind her. Afterwards Lucille approached the tutor and described the phenomenon to him. He was able to confirm that he had watched it too, but he did not explain it as she expected, in terms of a spiritual guide. Instead he said quite simply, 'That was her true Higher Self with her…'

It would seem, then, that we – the masters of ascension – are a mere whisker away from our long-awaited reunion.

CHAPTER 7

Remember who you are: being a master of light

How are you doing?

If you have read the chapters in this book in chronological order and you have just reached the end of the section on merkabahs and light bodies, how are you feeling right now? Be completely honest with yourself – are you really thinking of yourself as a master? Does the word and all that it implies sit easily with you? Do you have the confidence to use your remarkable abilities? Are your head and your heart in agreement?

Being a true master means enjoying our physical condition as well as nurturing ourselves spiritually. We have to learn how to walk that fine line between trusting the infinite and taking personal responsibility for our care and welfare.

If you went off on a spiritual tack but neglected to organise the basics such as paying the rent, it would hardly come as a surprise to you when you ran into problems.

This might seem self-evident, but some people do become so enchanted by their spirituality that they forget we are also here to have a human experience.

During my early working career I met a man who had been drawn to transcendental meditation. At first he meditated a few hours a week, but gradually it escalated until he was only content when he was meditating during every waking hour.

In his attempt to find an ideal space away from the illusion of the third dimension, he had the most marvellous visions which had great religious significance for him. But by this stage his meditation had become an addiction, and in the end he suffered a nervous breakdown. Stability returned when he recognised he had been concentrating on one part of his life at the expense of all the others.

It is rather an extreme example to give, but it is really just the flip side to the same coin minted by excessive workaholics and fitness fanatics – I can say that because I have been both simultaneously and have had some very tough lessons to learn!

The knack to balance in life is not taking your body for granted, but paying attention to it, heightening your senses where possible and in so doing raising your awareness of yourself and your surroundings. Through this will come an equal appreciation of inner and outer worlds and dimensions, and an understanding that being spiritual does not necessarily involve going into an altered state of consciousness. It is more a case of how you approach and cope with the challenges brought to you each day.

The ascended masters have moved beyond the need for reincarnation by demonstrating a clear understanding of these principles. If you would like to emulate them but you are not terribly sure how you are doing or whether you are up to it just at the moment, the following deceptively simple exercises may give you some helpful pointers. To get the real benefit, be truthful with yourself and treat them with a modest degree of seriousness. But above all, enjoy them, perhaps with a group of friends, and take from them what is appropriate for you.

If you seem to have more ticks than crosses in your imaginary progress box, always remember there is no such thing as failure and we do not have to be perfect to be masters. You need achieve only 51 per cent energy shift for each of your goals and by spiritual law the other 49 per cent will follow automatically. Your intent and dedication are more important than your so-called human frailties, so no matter how many times you apparently fall short of your aims hold your focus, love yourself and know you are probably much closer to your objective than you realise.

Set aside a quiet time for yourself – make sure you are out of reach of the telephone and that children or pets won't interrupt you. Find a pen, coloured pencils if you have them, and a large notepad – some people like a special notebook in which to jot down thoughts so that they have a record for the future. Put on your favourite relaxing music if that will help you to unwind and ask your higher self, angels, ascended masters, elemental friends or whoever you wish to involve to draw close to you for guidance and inspiration. Use the violet flame and then perhaps follow it by invoking the aquamarine ray for clarity.

When you feel settled, begin. You can obviously work through the exercises quickly in a single session if you want to, picking out those that appeal to you. However, the most rewarding way to approach them is to do them leisurely one at a time in the order they appear here. This may take longer, probably several sessions, but it will give you the opportunity to learn as much about your tremendous strengths as about areas you might address.

I am including for interest a few personal insights other people have gleaned for themselves from their own experiences of the exercises. So read each section all the way through first before going back and concentrating on the practical parts. Use the diagram overleaf to write notes/draw on directly, or copy it.

Exercise 1: Name calling

Say out loud ten times and then write down on a piece of paper the forename(s) you were given at birth. Now ask yourself these questions:

• do you like your name(s) and the sound of it/them? whether yes or no, why?
• do you still use it/them? if no, why?
• do you favour a shortened version of your name(s)? if yes, why?
• have you changed your name(s)? if yes, why?
• do you have a nickname? if yes, who chose it and do you really like it?
• do you have one version of your name(s) for friends and one for people you don't know? if yes, why?
• do you have unresolved issues connected to your name(s)? if yes, what are these?

Would it come as a surprise to learn that your name, or names if you have more than one, was chosen by your soul prior to incarnation? Before your spiritual essence was about to enter your

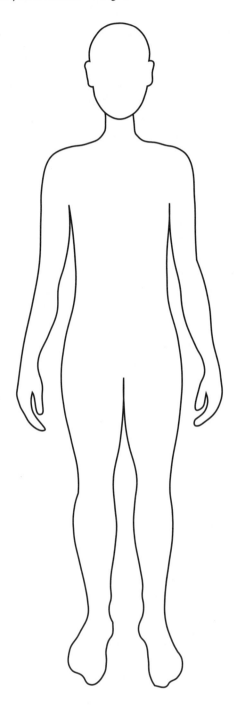

new body, your soul would have communicated telepathically its wishes to your parent(s) or guardians. It may have intended that the special resonances should bring suitable lessons to you. If you have had difficulties accepting your name, what challenges have you been presented with as a result and have you truly mastered them?

As a child, Gladys was told by a teacher at school that her name was old fashioned. She was naturally upset by this thoughtless remark when she was so young and literally took it to heart, for many years feeling uncomfortable with what she is called. But although the comment was hurtful at the time, she eventually came to understand that it was showing her how her perception of herself was actually bound up with her name. Once she admitted to herself that she had been using it as an excuse for not liking herself, and accepted that, her self-love blossomed and she now adores Gladys.

From the age of eight or nine Eleanor thought her name was akin to 'an enormously big weight that was too large to handle', and so she shortened it to 'Ella'. She sympathised with other people who use similar contractions, likening it to 'being under a stroking hand'. With a little encouragement she practised writing her full name on a piece of paper, and ended up by penning it with a great flourish (while doing this the right-hand side of her body was bathed in the violet ray, in support of her intent). She has since found that the longer Eleanor fits her well. Sometimes we just need time and confidence to grow gradually into our names and so into ourselves.

Names of course have their own vibrations that become interwoven with our personality, whose unique combination we and more particularly others can relate to. James can offer an interesting angle on this. He was born in Spain but now lives in Britain, and he likes to be called by his Spanish name when abroad and his English more or less equivalent at home. He acknowledges that whenever he reverts to Santiago he feels a very different person from the one he knows as James (formerly Jim!) This is partly because Santiago is used less often and its vibration has become less familiar to him; each time he re-adopts it he has to readjust to its frequency.

Perhaps one of your lessons is to discern which name is most appropriate for you, what resonates with your heart.

For example, if your childhood nickname has lingered into adulthood and you have outgrown it, be gentle but firm with your family and friends. Explain your current needs and ask that they be respected.

Some people assume an entirely different name from the one given at birth. They may be trying to escape the past, making an independent stand for themselves or, as in the case of Emerald, formerly Lynn, choosing a vibration more in keeping with their current level of spiritual development and work.

Friends may need a little time to adjust to an altered vibration, because the combined energies within names also become imbued with love. It can be doubly difficult for parents or teachers if children in their care suddenly decide to adopt a new alias. They may need to tread carefully while deciding whether it is just a whim or a clear direction from a child's soul as part of a life lesson. Invoke the yellow ray of wisdom and illumination if you ever find yourself in this situation.

Once you have thought about all the issues surrounding your forename(s), next consider your surname. Are you proud of your surname or would you have preferred something more distinguished? How have other people reacted to it? Were you teased at school? If you are a married woman, how did you deal with your husband's surname? Did you keep your maiden name in some form or were you happy with the change?

Think about your decisions and why you made them.

After I was married, I compromised. I used my married name whenever I was with my husband, but I kept my maiden name at work because my ego could not bear to be parted from it. 'White' was boring and there were lots of them in the staff directory! After leaving my job, however, I was forced to decide whether to continue being two people or the wholesome me my soul intended. I did the latter and dispensed with my maiden name. Much later I was pleased to discover that the letters in White, lovely symbol of purity, numerologically add up to the master number 11!

Having looked at your forename(s) and surname from all

angles, now put them together and repeat them out loud three times. How do you like the sound of the composition? Does it feel as though every element belongs to you and that you belong to it?

If you are uneasy, try to analyse why. Full acceptance of who you are includes being content with the harmonics of all your names.

Finally, as a way of completion to the exercise, say to yourself three times: 'I AM a Master and I love [insert your names here]. I AM Light and Love always.'

Exercise 2: Blessings from childhood

Write down on a piece of paper the place(s) where you were born and where you grew up, and think about the following:

• did you enjoy living where you did? whether yes or no, why?
• can you see the benefits from having lived in a particular area? if yes, make a list of them
• did you like the scenery, people, climate, etc? whether yes or no, why?
• did you choose to move away or did you stay? why?
• do you or would you like to visit? why?
• what life skills did you acquire? are you using them today?
• what lessons did you learn? can you see lessons from childhood repeating themselves now or have you dealt with them?
• are there any issues in your life which may stem from your surroundings when you were young?
• would it help to go back and lay ghosts to rest? if you can't get there physically, you can always travel in your mind; invoke the violet flame to heal the past.

In the same way that souls choose names, so they select times, dates and places of birth, as well as blood line/parents, families, lifestyles and cultures. During childhood we are presented with a wealth of opportunities to interact with our environment to find out about ourself and others. These experiences help us to lay down guidelines and patterns for the future, and are a very important part of our growth.

Even if you think you engineered a smooth transition from child to adult, make doubly sure there are no loose ends hanging free. Either weave them into your current life or call upon Archangel Michael to cut them off for you with his magnificent blue sword of truth and action. As long as you have attended to your own business from the past in the best way you can, this will remove old ties which other people for whatever reason may still be holding onto. You need to be free of them to move on.

Eta was born in Sumatra in the jungle. Her adventurous parents wished to make a go of plantation life, but this meant that their daughter spent much of her girlhood with no other children around for her to play with. She believes the isolation developed her self-reliance and resilience, qualities which have always served her well, especially when she had to face the severe tests of a Japanese prisoner of war camp during World War II.

Some people try to camouflage their origins by altering their accent and never going back 'home'. Others feel a cosy warmth when they revisit places they knew as a child and, like Louise, keep their regional dialect with pride.

During her early teaching days Louise was somewhat bewildered when a man who had appeared very friendly throughout a drama course came up to her at the end and rather brutally confided in her that he had never liked her because she was from the north of England (he was from the south). She also learned that, even though he needed the money, he refused to rent out his flat in London to anyone with the remotest northern twang in their voice.

Louise was perplexed by the man's irrationality. Throughout her teaching career she found that sticking to her verbal roots made her much more approachable and trusted than if, as she was encouraged to do at college, she had opted for elocution lessons to eradicate them.

Make a note of the strengths you have gained from being in the place(s) of your childhood. If you have a few grievances, list those too and work out a plan for transforming them into positive attributes. Bless your soul for its wise choices.

Exercise 3: My family tree

Draw a large tree and put the names of your family (or draw your relatives in whatever form takes your fancy) in amongst the branches and leaves, at the foot of the trunk or wherever you would like them to be.

Colour in some bright flowers and a gorgeous blue sky. If you have pets, perhaps you might like to include them too. Make the picture as beautiful as you can. When you are positioning your relations, think about whether your feelings towards them match the loveliness of your tree and whether you are happy for all of them to be part of your picture.

• Do you relegate some to the corner away from the rest or do you cluster them together in one festive grouping?
• How big have you sketched them? Are some larger than others?
• What emotions do you feel as you are drawing?

It is often said that you can choose your friends but you cannot choose your family. Since you now know that that piece of folklore is not true, why do you think your soul went to great lengths to place you with the people it did? What have you learned from them and what have you been able to teach them? Are they serving as mirrors, reflecting back to you aspects of yourself you like or dislike? Have you had to work through many tough issues which might hark back to previous lives together?

Ask forgiveness of anyone you may inadvertently or intentionally have hurt or wronged. If you cannot bring yourself to do it face to face, write them a letter or send them a gift or card with specially chosen words. Failing that, include them in your prayers and invoke the violet flame around each of you.

If you have relatives you just do not resonate with and who do not respond to you in a way which honours your individuality, send them love from your heart and get on with your life. Sometimes the timing is not right and the simplest solution is to let go and allow someone to be in their own space away from yours.

Exercise 4: I am me

Step 1

Draw in whatever way you can an honest picture of yourself. As you are doing this, ask yourself the following and keep a note of your thoughts:

- are you proud of your body and unafraid of showing its shape, or do you dwell on the bits you would rather were not there?
- do you wish you could change parts of your body?
- do you envy someone else's looks or hair?
- have your views about your body changed as you have grown older?
- are you still carrying negative thoughts about your body from when you were a child?

Reflect on why your soul might have chosen this particular body as your means of expressing your uniqueness. How do you treat it? With respect and love, or do you berate it from time to time for failing to live up to your expectations?

A lady attending a workshop talked about how she had been born without a breastbone. This made her look different from other people, but she had never let it bother her and she was leading a contented life. Her two children also had the same condition and, like their mother, had the option of undergoing a very complicated surgical procedure to give them a more conventional looking figure.

Her daughter had come to terms with her body and did not wish to alter it. Her son, however, was finding his soul's choice a tricky challenge and was seriously considering the operation. It was particularly difficult for him that both his mother and his sister had already accepted what nature had given them. The masculine part of him was fighting its corner.

When Joy was checking out the lessons her body had presented her with, she explained how embarrassed she had been at school. While her friends were dashing around 'all flat-chested and carefree', she had developed gorgeous feminine curves and, horror of horrors, periods, which she absolutely hated. She wanted to run from the way she looked and was.

Joy's life then produced a series of ailments that were specific to her gender, culminating in cancer of the cervix. Eventually she asked her soul why this had happened. To her astonishment the reply was, 'In your last life you were a man in a closed, religious order. And in this life you have chosen to experience *fully* what it means and how it feels to be a woman'.

Step 2

Draw another picture of yourself, this time highlighting in your favourite colours all that you love about your body. If there are still parts of you which you tell yourself are 'OK but…', colour those in too with pretty shades. Then write out the words '*I AM a Master*' with the same crayons. Stand back and admire the masterpiece which is you.

Step 3

Sit comfortably in a chair. Make sure your feet are flat on the floor, your knees are slightly apart and your hands are resting on your thighs or in your lap. Take three deep breaths and close your eyes. Gently relax and move your consciousness to within your body.

As you become more and more relaxed, send your consciousness to each part of you and find out where, if anywhere, you have discomfort. Really move into that place and ask yourself why the fear and/or pain is there. Surround areas that do not feel harmonious with violet and pink. Don't try to ignore them but accept them as part of you and begin integrating them into your whole being. Then expand your consciousness so that it fills your entire frame. Can you feel your hands, your feet, legs, torso, head, your heart beating? Finish by rubbing your hands together and opening your eyes. Stretch and give yourself a hug.

We have chosen to learn through a physical incarnation, so if we listen carefully to our bodies they will give us vital messages. If we can pick these up early enough, we can save ourselves much wasted time and effort in overcoming dis-ease. They may also give us pointers for our spiritual development.

When Angie did this exercise she felt pain in her back from having hurt it recently and also in one side and leg as she tried to compensate for the back problem.

When she analysed why she was experiencing difficulties in these areas of her body, she thought they related to what was happening, or in her instance not happening, in her life – she was reluctant to move forwards. It was suggested that because she senses a strong connection with angels she should ask them for healing. And since Louise had seen a large green energy in the room on the morning of the workshop, she hinted to Angie that she might call upon Archangel Raphael in particular.

That evening before going to sleep she did as advised. During the middle of the night she woke up and was amazed to feel heat down her side that was aching. She was also aware of a presence in the bedroom and knew that she had been talking to Archangel Raphael, although she could not remember what was said.

Cathy reported that for some reason she also had put her awareness on her back, and then images from childhood, ones she had not thought about for years, raced into her mind. She revealed that when she was young, health problems meant that she had to wear a brace. This in turn made it awkward for her to wear official school uniform or take part in sports; she was acutely self-conscious of her appearance. She even remembered an incident when a boy made a cruel joke about her and called her spiteful names.

Now recalling these events through a very simple body focusing exercise, Cathy was going through the process of releasing past trauma. Sometimes such energy blocks can be released via physical sensations – muscles may twitch and flutter. In whatever manner it happens for you, acknowledge the process and be grateful for it. You do not necessarily need to know what it all means as long as you can allow it to happen at its own pace.

Incidentally, Cathy chose to do this particular exercise in a garden in sunshine. When she closed her eyes she could see in her inner vision the outline in violet of another person standing very close to her.

While she could sense them, she could not immediately explain why they were there.

Sara reported that during her exercise she became aware of a sensation in her throat. After a few minutes of honest self-appraisal she admitted there were times when she knew she had to speak up but did not do so.

Developing this sort of awareness is about remembering who we truly are – we know deep down how to be the person our soul intends; it's just that we have forgotten the ways and means. Relearning and bringing skills to the surface can be easy if you give yourself time to tune in regularly to yourself.

With practice it will become automatic and you will know more or less immediately when your equilibrium is wavering.

Exercise 5: Am I all here?

Sit comfortably in your chair again, knees slightly apart, hands in your lap or on your thighs and feet flat on the floor. Close your eyes.

Concentrate on your breathing while relaxing and begin to use your inner awareness to discover whether you can sense all parts of you and whether there is symmetry and balance throughout your body:

- can you feel your limbs?
- does one arm feel heavier or lighter than the other, or do they feel the same?
- does each leg feel the same? can you feel your thighs, your knees, your calves?
- are you more aware of your front than your back or vice versa? do they feel connected?
- can you feel your feet on the floor?
- is one side of your body more comfortable than the other? can they 'talk' to one another?
- does your head feel connected to the rest of your body?
- do you feel grounded or 'floaty'?
- are there any bits of you that you cannot sense?
- affirm three times that you are committed to being in your body at this moment, and notice any difference in how you feel emotionally and physically.

Part of my own healing and spiritual growth has involved trying out a wide range of complementary therapies. Work with a polarity therapist, Liz, gave me huge insights into being fully present in my body.

The first time I visited her my physical energy levels were extremely low and when I saw the steep hill I thought I had to walk up to get to her, my heart sank. I wondered whether I would make it.

Nevertheless I set off, head down, and began my ascent. Just as I was about half way it felt as though my coat was pulled backwards with a jolt. I stopped, and when I looked up there was the entrance to a side alley along which was the door to Liz's rooms. I had been saved from getting lost and, more to the point, walking far further than was necessary.

Liz recommended some cranial treatment and I went along with her suggestion – during each session she insisted I should not just let things be done to me but that I should take responsibility for deciding what was in my best interests. That in itself was a helpful lesson.

As I lay on her couch with my eyes open but the rest of me miles away, I was brought out of my revery by a very pale blue pulsating colour that appeared above me. I happened to mention this to Liz, because it was distracting my attention away from what she was saying. She reported that at the very moment I opened my mouth to talk to her she had become aware of a spiritual presence. A few minutes later the colour changed to lilac and then it developed into a swirling sapphire blue cloud filling my entire field of vision.

Naturally I was fascinated by the phenomenon and even more intrigued by what Liz had to say about it. She explained that sometimes our spiritual essence goes part way out of our body, as a sort of self-defence mechanism. This can be the result of trauma, sometimes at or near birth, or as a way of keeping in touch with Spirit.

It can, quite understandably, become a habit. I thought about stressful occasions when I was 'in my head' but my brain did not seem to be in gear – as though I was watching and listening to someone else stumbling to find words; and my body could have been on another planet for all the awareness I had of being in it. Bells certainly began to ring for me.

Later sessions proved to me the truth of Liz's wisdom and being grounded became much less of an abstract concept. I would sit or lie in relaxed fashion, and Liz would ask me if I could sense, say, my legs.

The more I was truthful with myself and acknowledged a gap or emptiness if it were there, the more I recognised that my consciousness was shutting off access to much of my body. It preferred I was kept occupied by my mind, something I have probably done for much of my life to avoid dealing with pain in all its glorious forms! And probably my spirit has indeed heartily welcomed the opportunity to escape from time to time. But regular escapism is not really what living in the third dimension is all about.

When our masculine and feminine sides are in harmony with each other, when we are properly grounded here in the present in our body, and when we are balanced on physical, emotional, mental and etheric levels, we may feel more noticeably 'together' than usual, we comprehend what we are doing, our thinking is clear and our ability to verbalise is well honed. Our feet feel securely weighted down onto the earth. Knowing that nothing or no one can hurt us, the world is brighter and more beautiful than ever before. Our spirituality is everywhere.

Exercise 6: Believing is seeing

Step 1 – Using physical eyes
Find a place where you can sit or stand comfortably. Spend five minutes or so observing in minute detail all the objects you can see.

- what colour are the objects?
- where are they?
- what are they next to?
- what are they made from?
- do they have any associations for you?
- what do you most like about them?

It is easy to fall into the habit of looking at surroundings but not really taking them in. This exercise teaches us to remain focused and calm, and is a good preparation for meditation. If you find yourself in stressful situations which require a period of waiting, such as at the dentist's, soothe your nerves by breathing deeply, saying over and over again to yourself 'I AM a Master' and noticing all the positive aspects of your environment – colours, textures, messages (even if you do not relish the idea, you are fortunate to be having treatment), the people helping you, etc.

Step 2 – Using spiritual eyes
If Step 1 is about being focused, Step 2 is about being focused, alert and open at the same time. Believe and anything is possible – just because you may not yet have seen spiritual energy does not mean it does not exist!

Select an object (it could be inanimate or a person or animal) in front of you and look at that to the exclusion of everything else. Let your eyes go slightly out of focus and allow your awareness to move through the object, to the sides and up and down.

By maintaining this relaxed state, your 'spiritual eyes' (mainly your third eye and internal spiritual sensors within your brain working together) will be given the opportunity to pick up on extra-dimensional visual cues. You may notice a whitish haze round your object – its energy field – or you may see different colours. Use the 'I AM a Master' affirmation or invoke a ray, angel or ascended master to see whether it makes a difference to what comes into view.

Anyone who has perfected the art of finding the scenes in magic eye pictures will have a head start here. However, if you are one of those people who have never managed to pick out a dolphin from rows of roses, it does not mean you will not develop clairvoyantly! We all have the inherent ability, although some of us may have chosen not to use it this lifetime. And those who are very 'gifted' (I prefer this word to 'psychic') have an even greater responsibility to behave with the utmost integrity at all times.

Ken thought he would be hopeless at this exercise. But while other members of his group were busying themselves, he casually announced that he could make out a violet pyramid at the top of Louise's head (also noted by someone else; Louise was hold-ing a crystal at the time). Not only that, but he could also see vio-let mist swirling behind her, at her sides and in front of her. In other words he was watching her aura in 3-D. It was an earth-shattering moment for him and everyone else.

You might try looking at your hands against a pale or dark background. A lady who practises tai chi remarked that she often sees energy streaming out of people's hands while they are train-ing. Another woman noticed this on herself as well as a red colour coming from her right index finger (a palm reader might have been able to give some insight here). Yet another woman saw blue around her own fingertips and hands, a colour Louise once observed around a healer's hands.

Following the principle that there is usually a reason for what we are shown, Louise asked the lady if she too were a healer to which she replied that she would feel a fraud if she ever attempt-ed to do such a thing. She believed she did not have the ability. It was tactfully pointed out to her that she might consider using the 'I AM a Master' affirmation and be surprised at what she could accomplish if she transformed her thought patterns.

If you are with friends, you could play around with checking out everyone's full aura. When like-minded people gather together to learn and exchange views about spiritual matters, vibrations within and among them are raised many fold. This in turn can make it easier to sense energies – although it is not always the case for everyone.

Sally, who among many things channels sublime music from Archangel Michael (and featured so prominently in Louise's near death experience dream), was giving a talk one evening. To keep us alert and on our toes, she included a wonderful earthy blast on her didgeridoo.

When she was in full swing and the whole room was rever-berating to the instrument's fabulous deep resonances, her aura became flushed with red – denoting vibrancy and a strong con-nection with Gaia.

We certainly all felt recharged afterwards, our own auras no doubt having been showered with the magnificent sound and its colour.

Draw the outline of a human figure onto pieces of paper. Then take it in turns to stand in front of the group, preferably against a plain wall. Ask those observing to mark on the drawings any colours or other phenomena they see. It can be especially rewarding when several people pick up on the same features.

The first time I tried this with friends we were very pleased to be able to confirm with each other precise colours, even though we had never done anything like it before. One by one we sat in a special chair which our host informed us was strategically placed over an earth line that ran through the house. She thought it would amplify energy for us and make it easier for us to see it. She was proved right.

When I perched myself in the hot seat I watched the faces of all three of my observers simultaneously change their expression to one of utter amazement as a ball of energy apparently emerged from my left side, moved about a metre away and then went back into my body. I was oblivious to what they were witnessing but entertained by their wide eyes and open mouths.

During a similar exercise at Mandala several members noticed a bright energy high above and to Jeanette's left. We were doubtful about it being her aura, and Jeanette confirmed our suspicions: she is aware that one of her guides often assumes the very position we had remarked upon.

Bright sunlight and candlelight (and even artifical lights) may enhance some people's ability to see colours of fifth dimensional quality. This is probably due to the physical sun (or imitations of it) activating the third eye and pineal gland and in some way making it easier to connect spiritually with The Great Central Sun.

You might test this out for yourself:

• check out the area in and around a window whenever strong sunlight is streaming through it or get someone to stand in front of it and look for their aura
• glance at the sunlight (don't hurt your eyes by staring right into it!) or a candle flame, and then look away quickly. You might do this again and close your eyes after glancing away

• when you are sunbathing allow yourself time to soak in the warmth and rays; then, with eyes either closed or open, place a hand in front of your third eye. Also try covering your eyes.

Don't forget to use the 'I AM a Master' affirmation and violet flame invocation to support your intent. You will know when you have succeeded.

As a variation on a theme, you could close your eyes for a few minutes and ask your higher self, angels or ascended masters to show you the colours of your own aura – aura colours change according to how you feel, so if possible you will need to ask for a friend's confirmation straight away. You may be surprised at how accurate you can be. Just before having an aura photograph taken, Louise guessed hers to be green and violet. Moments later the developed film showed she was spot on.

You may find your physical eyes become tired easily the first few times you set your spiritual eyes working hard. This is quite normal. So don't overdo it – in fact close your eyes from time to time, and you may find colours entering your inner vision just the same. As with any activity, the more you practise, the more proficient you will become. Eventually you will feel no discomfort at all and your spiritual eyes will automatically be brought into operation when you need them – you won't even have to think about it: it will be as natural as glancing out of the window and admiring the scenery.

Once you have seen spiritual energy in a prescribed setting, you will then recognise it on other occasions when it is much more likely to arrive on an ad hoc basis. You will learn not to dismiss what you might earlier have construed as a trick of the light or a flight of fancy. The subtlest of energies will not escape your notice, and the more intense ones will be a revelation to you.

Exercise 7: Am I hearing things?

Step 1
Sit in your comfortable chair and assume the same position as before – feet flat on the floor, hands resting gently on your thighs. Close your eyes and take three deep breaths. Perhaps

invoke the violet flame to calm your mind from exercises you may have done beforehand.

Feel any stress melting away. Now centre your concentration on listening to what is going on outside the room. Can you hear birds singing or traffic going by? Does the noise jangle your nerves or are you feeling relaxed and contented? Spend five minutes enjoying being part of the wide world.

Step 2

Bring your concentration to within the room. What is going on there? You might be conscious of a clock ticking, a fire crackling, or a video recorder whirring round. Or are other people shifting position in their seats or breathing heavily?

Take time to make a mental note of the sounds and how you react to them. Are you irritated or detached? Then listen intently again until you become at one with them.

Step 3

Finally, bring your awareness to within your own body. Are your internal mechanisms audible to you? Are you embarrassed by them or do you feel at peace with yourself? Spend at least five minutes listening to your own unique rhythm and ignore the chatter of your mind. Send love to your body and thank it for everything it does for you.

This exercise is another excellent way of achieving calmness before meditation and is a natural precursor for working with the breath. However, like all these exercises, it can also throw up lots of surprises. When Hazell and her friends went through the different steps, the majority found number 3 gave them the most to talk about. Lucille said that as she listened to her body she simply heard a single musical note. Hazell asked her if she could play it on the piano, which she did. The note turned out to be A.

Then Aruna set the cat among the pigeons by enquiring whether the group wished to know what colour this note was. Of course everyone did, so she confidently informed them it was 'pale yellow' and, pointing to a bush through the window, 'like that rose in the garden, edged with gold'. Joy knew exactly what she meant, and agreed with her instantly. It would seem both of them were using their intuition to sense energy, something you can explore for yourself in Exercise 12.

As an aside, there are musicians who can compose music to match a soul's individual vibration. One such man, known as Neil H, will even work out the chord of someone's name and, if they have one, of its shorter version too. Sue was so bowled over by the richness, depth and quality of sound in her birth name that she promptly reverted to Susan and does not wish to return to its pale imitation ever again.

Music has probably the greatest capacity of any art form to raise or lower vibrations in and around people. So pause for a few seconds to think about your favourite pieces (do you listen to every bar or do you switch off until the best sections?) and then move on to other sounds that give you pleasure. Is there anything which gives you displeasure? Can you deduce why?

Josephine admitted that in the last twelve months she had developed an aversion to the clinking of pottery as it is placed in the dishwasher. She had no idea why it had only just become a nuisance for her. Was this another past life indicator? While she was talking, several people imagined her as a barmaid in a previous incarnation, handing out flagons of beer to leering customers. This colourful picture provoked laughter, but stranger things have been known...

Just as we have spiritual eyes, so we also have the ability to hear on a spiritual frequency. Again, intent, attentiveness and openness are the keys to developing this ability. It has been said many times before in spiritual circles and is worth repeating here once more: although other people's starting point may appear to be more advanced than yours, never fall into the trap of comparing your perceived inadequacies with their supposed successes. You have all you need to be who and what you wish to be, and the sort of contact you have with other dimensions will be wholly appropriate for you. (If you ever hear high pitched ringing noises, it may be due to the higher realms making adjustments from their side of the fence to assist you.)

The way Hilda's spirit friends communicate with her can be both baffling and on occasion very helpful. She has lost count of the number of times she has wandered up an empty aisle in a supermarket and heard her name called out. She always makes a point of checking whether there is someone in the vicinity who knows her, but invariably there is no one around. And whenever she oversleeps she is grateful for the loud bangs which rouse her without fail on time.

It is not uncommon for people to hear their name spoken, so if it happens to you you might like to take the opportunity to establish some sort of dialogue, even if it is just greeting them (you don't have to speak out loud) or asking who it is that is attracting your attention. A word of caution: you do not have to pursue communication if you do not wish to, and if you do it is always advisable to check your contact has your highest interests at heart (see page 176 for more about this).

Gerry had extreme presence of mind when he was unexpectedly paid a visit by one of his guides while he was driving his car. He was on his way to an exam; the sun was shining and although it was a long time since he had had to do a test of this sort he was perfectly laid back about it. Then, in an instant, it felt as though his body had been moved backwards and another person was at the wheel – and not driving particularly well!

After this sensation came three visions in quick succession: the first was of a male Innuit wrapped in an animal skin; the second was a close-up of a pair of almond-shaped eyes; and the third was a snow scene. Gerry did not hesitate and requested the presence make itself known. He caught the word 'Lakachuk' and assumed it was a name. He repeated it, awkwardly at first, and sensed laughter at his poor pronunciation. From that day onwards Gerry felt compelled to discover more about Lakachuk and did not rest until he eventually established a closer link with his guide whom he now channels (for more on channelling see Chapter 8).

Another aspect of listening is tuning in to your own inner wisdom. You probably already do so instinctively, especially during emergencies – minor or major. But you can also draw on your intuition, higher self or whatever you wish to call it in more controlled settings. The next time you meditate, ask yourself a question beforehand and wait for the answer during your period of deep relaxation. Try not to second guess by letting your mind or ego chatter away while they work on a solution. If you can keep anxiety at bay and remain still, words or feelings may come to you out of what seems like nowhere, totally unrelated to what you may have been half consciously suppressing at the time.

Whenever I have used this technique it is as though the answer comes right up from my boots – which in itself is intriguing, because it is clearly distinct from thoughts generated by my mind which usually seem to emanate from my head and loving responses which come from my heart. (See Chapter 8 for more about the importance of linking with your higher self.)

Christine recalls an afternoon when she was very upset and had gone to sit by a river to reflect on her situation. She was confused, emotionally hurt and did not know which way to turn. She must have called out in some way for guidance and after a while she describes what was not so much a voice as an inner knowing or feeling that came to her. She translated it into the words 'These are man's laws, not God's.' This different perspective, which she had not considered before, brought immense comfort to her.

We are all given a host of messages and gifts from the universe each day. If we are swamped by emotions we may miss many of them, but if we can practise balancing ourselves from our hearts and learn to recognise the signals our lives can be greatly enriched.

Step 4

As a last step in this exercise, how do you feel about the sound of your own voice? Sing a couple of verses of a well-known song or lah any tune that comes into your head. Do you feel comfortable or embarrassed? Did someone once tell you you couldn't sing and so you haven't let rip in the vocal chord department since?

Invoke the violet flame around your throat area before enveloping it with pink and love. Then really sing your heart out. It can be a liberating and healing experience if you have never allowed yourself to express yourself freely in this way before – God's choir is not complete without your voice.

Exercise 8: What's that smell?

For this exercise rummage round your bathroom, bedroom, kitchen, meditation room, garden, etc to gather together a selection of scented products.

Don't overwhelm yourself with too many, but choose maybe five of your favourites. Then sit down, and first of all make a list of the smells you actively do not like. Why is this – do they have bad associations for you?

Now turn your attention to each of your items, enjoying their perfumes and explaining to yourself why you find them so attractive. Are they uplifting, soothing, reminiscent of good times?

Aromas, like music, can be exceedingly evocative and can swiftly bring a place, person or situation to mind. Can you gauge from your reactions to those you are currently thinking about whether you have mastered lessons they might represent? Is there anything from the past you could do with releasing?

A woman could not tolerate a particular brand of soap because it reminded her of morning sickness during her pregnancy. The soap in itself was probably harmless enough, but it may have symbolised changes in her body she found distressing. Was she therefore projecting emotions she had not really dealt with onto an external object? What would happen in the future if circumstances dictated she stay in a house or hotel where the only soap available was the one she had an aversion to?

Fragrances can also be associated with spiritual dimensions too, so do not automatically assume a scent you come across unexpectedly originates from an earthly source. Lavender is commonly linked by mediums with people who have passed over, as well as tobacco. When Louise was on the train to Hazell's after Hazell's husband had died, she detected the strong aroma of his favourite pipe tobacco. And wafts of her father's pipe are often noticed in her living room at home. They are lovely calling cards, a nice way of dropping by and saying hello.

If you have had no previous experience of spiritual essences or energies, never limit yourself and assume this is always going to be the case. One night at Mandala Christine smelt roses very strongly and had the image of Mother Mary encircled by roses impressed upon her. She did not say anything about the distinctive scent, and no one else commented either. Just as people were leaving, Louise heard a few words of a Beatles song – 'Mother Mary comes to me' – pop into her head.

Later in conversation with Christine she happened to mention this because she felt the quite specific phrase must have been important. Christine was taken aback, explained what she had experienced and then said, 'I'm usually the one who doesn't hear or sense anything!' This particular incident confirmed that that might not be the scenario for the future.

Exercise 9: Feeling good

Walk round the room touching objects and compare how they feel to your fingertips and in your hands. If you have a friend with you, get them to pass you things while you close your eyes. Can you recognise what you are holding? Is the sensation pleasurable or does it set your teeth on edge? Can you establish why?

If you have access to a garden or natural area outside and the weather is fine, stroll round and do the same there. Are you aware of a breeze blowing against your face? Is the grass short and tufty or springy? Are the leaves on the trees soft or brittle? Can you walk bare foot on the ground? Beyond a natural reaction to sharp points, are you comfortable doing this or does the strangeness unnerve you? Are you confident being you in your chosen body in your chosen environment?

After you have explored your surroundings, single out a space, inside or out, where you can spend a few more moments in silence. Breathe deeply and put your hands together, palm to palm, in front of you. How does it feel?

A group of friends might pair up, with each couple facing one another and doing the same, though this time they should place their hands against their partner's. How do you all feel about the contact? Do you sense a combined oneness or have your individual spaces been invaded?

Think of life in general: is each of you accepting of other people entering your aura or are there instances when you prefer to keep your distance?

A number of portable stress-busters can be small objects to hold, squeeze or throw between the hands. My grandmother had 'worry eggs', beautiful pieces of alabaster carved to the size and shape of duck eggs. They were cool and smooth as glass to the touch, and were intended to be handled when you felt uptight – although I always worried about dropping and breaking them!

Some people stroke a pet's silky smooth coat to re-establish their poise, whereas others might rub their hands against their thighs or face. It has actually been shown that keeping someone's hands away from any part of their body for a period of time causes them to become terribly disorientated. You might find, therefore, that putting yours palm to palm is a good way of doing the opposite, of rebalancing yourself. Experiment to find out what works best for you.

Our sense of touch is yet another means through which powerful spiritual messages can be conveyed. I used to work with a caring, sensitive man known fondly as Stevie. He is a Buddhist and is following his path with great dedication. Shortly after his father died he was meditating one evening, trying to come to terms with the events of the past few weeks, when he felt the sensation of a hand gently slipping into his and holding it. He did not elaborate further on the experience when he related it to me the next day, but I suspect the loving gesture was very gratefully received.

Exercise 10: Food for life

• do you taste food when you eat it?
• do you chew your meals or do you tend to wolf them down?
• do you give yourself plenty of time to enjoy each meal of the day?
• do you take food and drink for granted or are you regularly thankful for these gifts?
• does your body have cravings for certain tastes/types of food and drink? do you listen to them carefully to hear the real messages behind them or do you ignore them but still try to satisfy the cravings in any way and as often as you can?

- what are your likes and dislikes? do these say something about you?
- do you eat to live or live to eat?
- are you allergic to or intolerant of certain food/drink ingredients? have you worked out from a spiritual perspective why this might be so?
- do you give yourself plenty of spiritual nourishment (e.g. books, courses, meditation, time for reflection, meeting regularly with like-minded people)?

The fifth of our senses, taste, can be the one we think about least in spiritual terms, and yet it can be a useful marker, pointing out for us aspects of ourselves that might be tipping the scales on more than just the physical level. Food and drink are very personal choices, which ideally should reflect our unique bodies and their requirements. By this I mean that not every diet or slimming regime is suitable for every person.

A friend of my mother decided she would put herself on a special diet in the hope it would alleviate her arthritis and diabetes. She bought *the* book on the subject and rigidly followed the author's advice. Within a few months she had not only lost several kilos but her symptoms were vastly improved, leaving her able to resume the weekly dancing she had feared she would have to give up for good.

She was so impressed by the results that she insisted her husband should reap the benefits of the special diet too. After a few weeks, however, his already thin frame was reduced to stick-like proportions. His body did not need the recommended foods and their combinations; it was perfectly all right with what he had been eating before.

As your body becomes filled with increasing amounts of light and your cellular structure changes, you may find yourself compensating for this by homing in on certain foods that will give you the nutrients you require at this time; your tastes may alter and you may get by on less food than you used to.

Louise's son Alexander has never seen much point in eating very much and as a young boy could not understand why we do not just go outside and breathe in our nourishment instead.

What an enlightened child! Even today he thrives solely on peanut butter sandwiches, a few chips and chocolate, and he never has hot drinks.

As Alexander was growing up this created tension among members of the wider family, who intimated that Andy and Louise were not raising their son properly. However, without knowing about his diet, someone once helpfully shed some light on the matter for them. They were told that he had been in a Russian famine in a previous life. This might go some way to explaining his current minimal needs.

There are some people who, like St Germain apparently, can really exist entirely on light and who depend only on energy, also known as prana or chi, from The Source to sustain their physical bodies. One such lady, Ilona, who has lived on light for months, thought she ought to make sure she was not inadvertently causing herself harm by not eating. She asked for medical checks to test her bone density, blood and the like, and the results showed her to be in excellent health.

To live on light requires an acclimatisation period and during hers Ilona experienced cravings for certain types of food. But she soon realised it was not the actual food she wanted but the taste of it. On the odd occasion she ate anything at all, no more than a few mouthfuls now and then, she was very sensitive to the energy vibrations of her snacks. She was particularly affected by freshly harvested organically-grown salads which seemed 'bubbly' in her mouth. You can imagine how dense and heavy other inorganic, processed foods tasted!

If you don't go in for organic ingredients, you can always prepare your dishes with a loving heart and a whirl of the violet flame instead. This will bring out the energetic best in meals.

Exercise 11: Breath of life

Sit quietly in your chair and close your eyes. Imagine you are surrounded by tiny stars of light which flash and sparkle all around you. There are millions and millions of them, each lit from the heart of The Source and bursting with love. Now breathe in deeply through your nose, inhaling a shower of stars – some shoot into your lungs and some upwards into your head. As you exhale, cascade them outwards into your arms and downwards into your abdomen, legs and feet. Do this several times.

On the next few breaths send the stars through your blood vessels to every organ of your body, including your skin, feeling them energising your cells. Continue breathing in the golden stars until you sense an equilibrium inside and outside you. It is as though you are inhaling and exhaling stars of equal brilliance.

Once you feel balanced, open your eyes and sit quietly for a couple of minutes. Contemplate your breathing patterns during the day:

- do you always try to sit or stand in a way which makes it easy for you to breathe easily?
- do you clench your diaphragm? (people may do this when hiding emotions, sometimes experienced a long time ago)
- do you breathe shallowly? (this can be a form of self-protection or a way of avoiding coming to terms with emotional upsets)
- do you consciously take time out during the day to breathe deeply for a few minutes?
- do you use deep breathing to help centre yourself?

We do not all have to live on light in the same way as Ilona to benefit from The Great Central Sun's energy. Every time you breathe in you are taking in spiritual nourishment, so the more freely you do so the greater amount of divine energy will circulate within you. Deep breathing strengthens the body and focuses awareness – it is recommended before stressful events and is used by some healers during therapy.

There are also advocates of controlled breathing exercises, although some of these can be a little complicated to learn. While they do produce impressive results on many levels for studious practitioners, they do not appeal to everyone. So if you like to keep things simple, spend a couple of minutes three times a day filling your lungs with good clean (if you can) air. Stand with your feet apart, and imagine drawing the air in through your feet and hands too. Notice how empowering this is. Not only does it aid digestion, it will make you feel in control of yourself.

You can use breathing techniques in awkward situations as well. For instance, if you have to attend meetings where the debates tend to become rather heated, concentrate on your breathing and say to yourself something along the lines of 'I AM a Master. I take in Light' with each inhalation and 'I send out Love' with every exhalation. Expect rapid improvements in atmosphere.

Exercise 12: Sensing energy

Step 1
Sit in a comfortable position, and let your mind wander off on its own for a few minutes:

- what thoughts come to you?
- do they provoke an emotional response? If so, is this positive or does it leave you feeling less than centred?
- are your thoughts generated by fear or by love?

Now spend five minutes quietening your mind. Imagine you are holding a huge golden eraser to rub out images and words that come into it. Or you might prefer a massive hair drier with which to blow them into the Light. As they become fewer and fewer, put the eraser or drier to one side and visualise yourself softly puffing them away – you might even do this physically: inhale through your nose and then, as you exhale through your mouth, breathe away the flotsam. Continue until you can breathe in and out through your nose only. You already know it, but now truly believe it: mental, emotional and physical stability brings a greater spiritual connection, and paves the way for interdimensional experiences.

Whenever you enter a room where people have argued recently, the expression 'you could cut the air with a knife' is usually quite apt, isn't it? Body language will obviously tell you a great deal, but even without that your senses will pick up on the field of dense energy that was generated by the thoughts, words – unspoken as well as spoken – and emotions of those quarrelling. It is literally like walking into a brick wall.

If you are with friends, you could experiment with creating for yourselves different energy fields and finding out whether you can detect them. Ask one person to leave the room and go to another where the group cannot be heard. The rest of you should then sit in a circle and decide which particular emotion you are going to concentrate on. You can all think about it and/or express it – for humour or joy, for instance, simply have fun telling each other jokes.

Whoever has not been part of the group mind meld (take it in turns) should return to the room at a predetermined time, step into the space within your circle and, using their intuition, tune in to the energy. Invite them to talk about anything they sense – this could be a warmth, a coolness, a thought that comes into their head, an ache in their body.

No matter how small a reaction, encourage them to share their experience. Always invoke the violet flame afterwards to cleanse the room and yourselves, especially if you have been focusing on lower density emotions such as fear and dislike.

Having an understanding of your power to create high- or low-level energy by even the most fleeting of thoughts or casual of remarks is another element of your mastery. Learn to identify with only that which serves to lighten yourself and others, and you will increasingly draw to you more of the same.

Step 2
Select five objects with which to practise sensing energy. These might include a crystal, a potted plant, a piece of fruit, a wooden bowl, an original painting, an inspirational book. Take several minutes with each of them, placing one hand, then the other (and both together if the object is large enough) roughly 5 cm away.

Can you feel anything? If so, what? Alter the distance between your hand(s) and the items. Does this make a difference?

You may not sense anything, and that is perfectly fine. Give yourself a few minutes more and try not to become impatient – still your mind, use the 'I AM a Master' affirmation and make a note of whatever enters your head. Awareness of energy can come through any of your senses, so allow your intuition to work in whatever way is best for you. Some people get a tingling sensation in their hands; others feel a warmth; and yet others find a coolness. In one instance a man received the impression from a rose that he was 'crowding its space' as he brought his hands closer in towards it.

Step 3
This time find as many objects as you can to represent the colours of the rainbow and/or the twelve celestial rays. As in Step 2, use your hands to ascertain any differences between them. Try closing your eyes for the exercise. Is it easier? How do you sense the energies? If there are clothes among your items, how do you feel in the different colours? Place each against your face: how do you react?

With your eyes open, are you especially drawn to one or more colours? Do they call you to them? Do you feel a profound connection? The answers may point you towards the ray(s) on which you are contracted this lifetime. Double check by asking yourself whether you resonate with the divine qualities represented by the colours.

Another option is to close your eyes, ask for guidance from your I AM presence and the ascended realms, and pass your hand(s) over the objects until you sense intuitively to stop. The colour of the item you have selected may be the confirmation you have been seeking. (You may need to do this more than once if you are working with several rays.)

If you are not drawn to any colour in particular, review the lessons you have had in life. Do you notice patterns? Which of your attributes have been brought to the fore most often to deal with them? Try to think laterally – don't necessarily jump to the most obvious answers.

For example, if you were having problems with romantic relationships and had not yet found that perfect partner, it might not be that your ability to create abundance for yourself (green ray) was under scrutiny. You might in fact have needed to love yourself fully first before you could make things work with another person. So your ray would be pink.

When Louise presented a piece of aquamarine coloured paper to a workshop, several people commented on how it gave them 'a tummy wobble'. One man felt a similar sensation with magenta paper. He thought about why he might have had this reaction, and decided it represented a clash of vibrations or change of energies. He was going through a transition period in his life which he described in terms of out with the old and in with the new. And he recognised he was also beginning to move away from dark coloured clothes, which he had always worn in the past, to lighter ones.

As another part of the exercise, Louise dropped scarves one at a time into the lap of each person and asked them to guess, without looking, what colour they were. Without even touching them a woman knew in her mind straight away which was which, and marvelled at her new-found ability. Another lady used her intuition to guess the colours correctly but then allowed her logical thought processes to intervene; much to her irritation, they talked her out of her correct hunches.

After Linda used the 'I AM a Master' affirmation, she fancied one colour but then the word 'fuschia' strongly came to mind. She went with that and she was absolutely right. This reminded her of another instance when her intuition sprang into action. Her son and daughter-in-law were expecting a baby, and everyone had convinced themselves it was going to be a girl.

Early one morning Linda woke up to the name 'Matthew' resounding three times in her head. She wondered what it meant, but did not have to wait long to find out. Her son rang later that same morning to tell her the exciting news that she was now the proud grandmother of his baby son whom they were intending to call… Matthew.

When Jeanette was given a scarf, she felt a beautiful undulating energy and was shocked when she opened her eyes and saw it was green. A Romany had once recommended that she should avoid wearing green and so, because she respected him, she had followed his advice ever since.

This raised once again the question of clothes, their colours and how we can be affected by them. You can benefit from absorbing some of a colour's vibration, which is useful to remember first thing in the morning when you are deciding what to put on – tune in to how you are feeling and select accordingly.

On the other hand you may allow prejudices to affect your judgement. For example, some people cannot bear to have anything which resembles the shades (and often textures!) of their school uniform. Others believe black should always be worn to traditional functions – one woman declared that although she likes yellow, she would never ever wear it to a funeral.

When questioned about this, she retorted, 'Well, it's not done, is it?' But as she confronted herself on this issue, she sighed, 'Oh dear! Oh yes! Oh no! I think I know what I've said!' She agreed that as a master she could enjoy the freedom of being true to herself and could indeed wear whatever colour she wanted to a funeral.

One last point here: it is not unusual for some people to think of days of the week, numbers, names and even music as colours. I believe the technical name for this is 'synaesthesia', but I also view the phenomenon as the means by which individuals read and translate energies into what is most helpful for them.

It could therefore be construed as another example of intuition coming to the fore and demonstrates how there are myriad ways you can exploit your sixth sense. It is just a question of learning your own unique signals and paying close attention to them.

Step 4 (for two or more people)
(a) Working in pairs, use your hands and/or dowsing rods to sense each other's aura, starting close to the body and moving outwards in stages. Write down your findings:

  • when using your hands, what physical sensations do you feel?
  • can you determine the extent of the aura?
  • is it even all the way round or does it fluctuate?
  • does it feel stronger in certain places?
  • do your rods react in the same way at each of the measuring stages? (it has been known for rods to remain parallel on one

The energy of St Germain, as channelled specially for this book by Graham Cheater. The picture contains many powerful healing symbols, including the violet flame and the touching triangles of spirit and matter

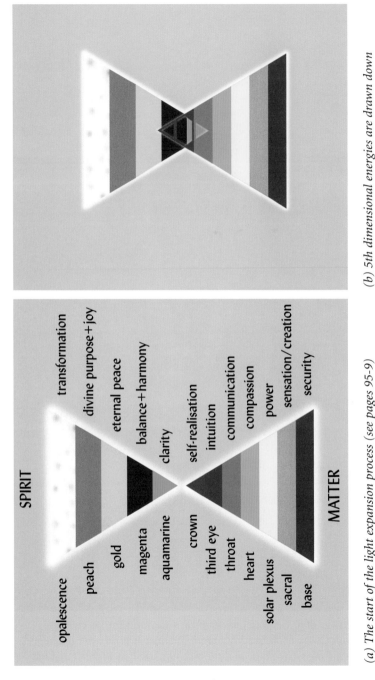

SPIRIT

MATTER

transformation
divine purpose+joy
eternal peace
balance+harmony
clarity
self-realisation
intuition
communication
compassion
power
sensation/creation
security

opalescence
peach
gold
magenta
aquamarine
crown
third eye
throat
heart
solar plexus
sacral
base

(a) The start of the light expansion process (see pages 95-9)

(b) 5th dimensional energies are drawn down

(d) Completion: the two interlocked triangles have rotated, creating the merkabah – a vehicle of light and colour

(c) Spirit and matter have now joined and locked. The next crucial step in the process is a 180° turn or 'flip' of the whole

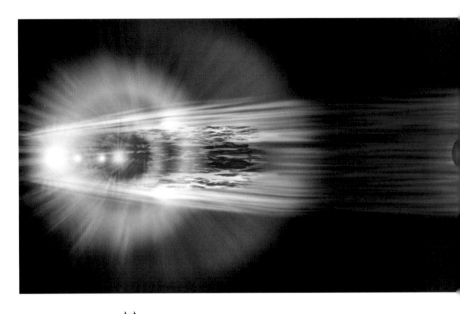

I AM a Master of Light

Graham Cheater's magnificent interpretation of the divine self (see page 186). Using the suggested invocations will help you along your ascension path – merging first with your Christ consciousness (figure surrounded by blue) and ultimately with your I AM presence or soul (top image)

I call to me the Light
and Love of my Higher Self

I invoke the Violet Flame to
transmute energy in and
around me and
transform it into Light

I AM a Divine Being of Light
living in a physical body

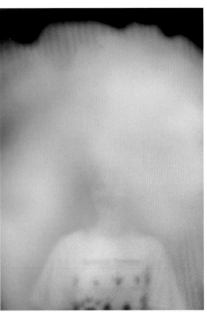

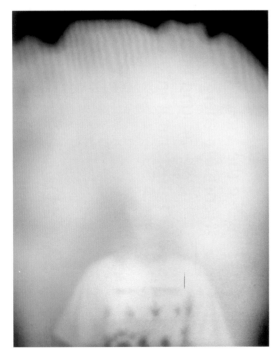

Jane's aura photographs
(1) Top left: Before invocations
(2) Top right: A few seconds after saying the affirmation, 'I AM a Master' (see pages 64 and 185) – the aura is beginning to clear
(3) Left: After calling on whoever had been involved with the book. The clear division of colours (blue, pink and gold – colours of the three-fold flame) suggested recent merging with the Christ consciousness – see page 186

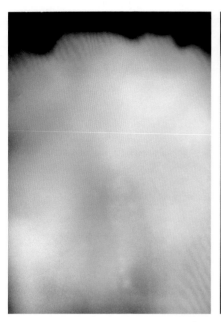

Louise's aura
photographs
*(1) Top left: Starting
point before invocations*
*(2) Top right: After the
violet flame invocation
(see pages 71 and 185) –
the effect on the aura
was immediate and very
striking*
*(3) Right: After the
invocation, 'I AM now
calling to me the energies
which have been
working with me on this
book'. Is this an example
of 'overlighting' by the
ascended masters (see
page 188)?*

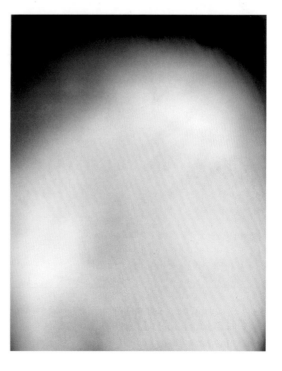

A drawing (perhaps representing the 12-strand Atlantean DNA, as well as our transformational future DNA) which Paul channelled from his higher self (see pages 122 and 188)

side of the body and to swing to left and right in a wavy
pattern on the other side)
• can you tell when your partner is sensing your aura? if so,
how?

(b) If there are several of you, form a circle and ask one person
to stand in the centre with their eyes closed. Then take it in turns
to approach the 'piggy in the middle' silently until you are only a
short distance away. Ask the piggy to guess who is standing near
(can they recognise any particular energy pattern or signature?)
and the reasons for their decision.

This naturally works best if everyone knows one another rea-
sonably well. If they don't, you may need to organise a form of
introduction beforehand. Just shaking hands can enable you to
gauge each other pretty accurately.

Have you ever met someone for the first time and felt an
instant bond? If so, you may have known them in a past life or
you may have picked up on a fellow soul group member's vibration.

Rather like people from similar geographical areas bonding
together because they have shared experiences of places and even
friends, you can tell immediately when you are with a spiritual
counterpart even though you have not come across them before.
You will also respond to anyone whose divine lightness is similar
to yours – they really are on the same wave length as you.

To be able to distinguish between different energy patterns
and high and low vibrations is an important element of discernment, and will serve you in good stead when you connect with
beings in other dimensions.

(c) Retaining the circle formation, dowse for the outermost
points of the piggy's aura. This may help to confirm details from
(a).

When Louise did this series of exercises at Hazell's as part of a
trial workshop, it turned out to be a very powerful and moving
event. At the start Hazell invited each person to select an angel
card and to relate it to the day's proceedings. She took hers and
peered rather quizzically at it. She shrugged her shoulders and

showed it to Louise. Louise agreed that its theme was not one she would immediately have associated with her – she surely had dealt thoroughly with its issues already.

As the day wore on Hazell forgot about the angel card. Then came the dowsing exercise and she happily stood in the centre of the room while everyone else formed a circle around her. It took only one step forwards from members of the group for their dowsing rods to cross, showing that Hazell's aura extended roughly 1.5 metres out from her body. All that is, apart from one person.

He moved forwards another step, and another, and yet another, until he was just two thirds of a metre away on her left side before his rods crossed. To make sure this was not an error, the exercise was repeated several times with different people assuming the position on Hazell's left. It proved not to be a mistake and Hazell's worried expression soon brought reassurances from Louise who quickly started to analyse the situation. The left represents the past, so she gently enquired whether there was anything from Hazell's past which she was holding on to. No, there wasn't. Perhaps, then, she continued, part of Hazell's energy had gone from her at some point, maybe through illness.

Hazell gasped at this suggestion, because it straight away brought back memories of a stroke she had suffered on her left side the year before. At the time she had delved into the emotional reasons for it and had, as far as she was concerned, resolved them. Thanks to the immediate attention of a homeopath she had made a swift physical recovery, but it seemed that further healing on a different level was now called for.

The next steps taken by the group were all done instinctively – Louise invoked the violet flame and put her hands on Hazell's shoulders, another person visualised golden light, and the rest beamed out love to her. Amidst these ministrations Hazell dissolved into tears and realised with shock that she was releasing pent up emotions. Then, suddenly, it was all over. She grabbed a tissue, composed herself, and explained how extraordinary the experience had been.

At that moment she remembered her angel card from the morning. It had been, most appropriately, the card of healing.

Exercise 13: Dusting off daily routines

To finish this section, now might be a good time to mull over the
spiritual affirmations, invocations, decrees, prayers, rituals, etc
you do or say regularly. Spend a few moments thinking about
them:

- are they still right for you?
- do you still need them?
- is it time to stretch yourself a little further spiritually?
- do you have enough time for your spiritual practices? if not,
what can you do to improve matters for yourself?
- do you have plenty of good intentions but never seem to
follow them through?
- do you have a daily routine or do you often end up
snatching a few minutes when you can?
- are you frustrated by constant interruptions?
- do you feel every word from your heart or do you find
yourself repeating things parrot fashion?
- are you prepared to give the 'I AM a Master' affirmation and
violet flame invocation a go regularly?

Many people have a good idea about what spiritual practices
work for them and do their best to incorporate them into their
lives as much as possible – on the way to work, while ironing,
having a bath, walking the dog…

Having said that, it's very easy to slip into comfortable routines; months can pass by in the blink of an eye and you may still
find yourself automatically using the same affirmations you
introduced the year before.

As you are constantly evolving and changing, you owe it to
yourself to ensure you are aiming towards as high a vibration as
you can possibly manage. This may mean keeping some affirmations, dispensing with others, and bringing in new ones; trying
different meditations; letting go of anything which does not
serve your higher purpose.

If you can, give a little extra thought now and then to how
you can maximise the best use of the tools and time available to
you.

If spiritual rituals do not feature regularly for you because they are not your thing or you lead a hectic life and you have family commitments, you might consider the benefits to be gained by taking only a few moments at the beginning of each day for one or two prayers.

While people often feel frustrated at not being able to set aside large amounts of special time just for themselves, it is generally agreed that even a couple of minutes of positive thought early in the morning sets the tone for the rest of the day.

One last thought – the best, simplest and most effective ritual of all is always to act, speak and think from the heart. Funny how it can be the hardest to perform!

CHAPTER 8

Connecting with ascended masters

Louise had been invited to a spiritual awareness group to give a talk on the ascended masters. She packed her bags in the usual way, and drove some distance to her contact's house. When Harry, whom she had never met before, opened the door and welcomed her, there was a faintly startled expression on his face. Louise instantly knew he had been expecting someone very different, and wondered who he had had in mind.

While they were sipping cups of tea, waiting for Harry's wife to return, Louise discovered he had assumed from their telephone conversation that she was 65 and white haired. As she was still 40 something with chestnut coloured hair, she was rather amused by this. She took it all in her stride, and they joked about the wisdom she must have conveyed in her voice.

His next comment was less easy to circumnavigate. 'Of course you'll be channelling tonight, won't you?' he said, at which point she gulped. Whatever had he been told about her? While she and I had tried to 'channel' on our own, nothing as far as we were aware had ever happened (although in retrospect our expectations at that time had probably been rather naive and limited).

She thought carefully for a few moments and responded with, 'Channelling can be looked at in different ways.' Then she added with a laugh, 'I'll tell you now – there won't be funny voices or anything like that! But I do know there are times when words come out of my mouth and later I wonder where they came from and what I actually said because I can't remember.'

She was challenged again on the same subject after her talk. A woman in the audience asked, 'Are you channelling? Where do you get your information from?' Louise repeated similar sentiments she had expressed earlier to Harry. A second person then spoke up: 'I'm surprised by what you say. From the energy

around you – I see two beings – I feel you're overshadowed.' Not
having come across this phrase before in her own context, Louise
stored the episode in her memory for us to debate later. It raised
issues we needed to clarify for ourselves.

Having talked to people who call themselves channels,
watched, learned, read, listened, experimented and along the way
undergone some fascinating information-garnering experiences
of our own, we now feel able to answer questions on a subject
that can often be misconstrued.

Probably the most important point to make first of all,
though, is that you do not have to channel ascended beings to be
a master – if you are not drawn to it, that is absolutely fine. It is
not to everyone's taste, and nor is it part of everyone's learning
curriculum this lifetime.

However, a strong link with your higher self, your very Godself, is definitely worth cultivating. As current general interest
still lies predominantly with channelling energies from the fifth
dimension and above, I will concentrate on that for the most
part. But I will return at the end of the chapter to what I have
hinted at and tried to encourage throughout the book and which
I can promise will eventually become an irresistible topic for
you.

What is channelling?

Basically, channelling is the act of expressing in some way information, knowledge, creative impulses, feelings, visions,
thoughts, healing, sounds, music, etc received directly from the
ascended realms.

In other words it is a form of communication, like mediumship, which depends on the individual, their needs and assign-
ments, and how best their physical body translates spiritual data
inputted on high level frequencies. There is no real mystery as
such: it is a natural part of spiritual development and opportunities usually present themselves when the time is right to begin
exploring in this area.

Some people who would not necessarily call themselves spiritual nevertheless channel the higher dimensions unknowingly,

bringing through state of the art design or innovative technology in their work. Others, in contrast, are very aware when it is
happening and take active steps to build a relationship with
ascended masters. Examples of how you can do this will be discussed shortly.

In some circles it is assumed that to channel properly you
have to be able to repeat words whispered in your ear by a well-
known ascended master to an assembled crowd. This really is not
the case. Verbal channelling (see page 179) to groups certainly
has its place, and is an excellent way of conveying learning to
large numbers of people in one go. But it is not appropriate for
everyone. And it is not the only way of channelling.

Have you ever been in a desperately sticky situation in which
you had to speak or act quickly? Did you find yourself, like
Louise, opening your mouth and listening to an outpouring of
words you did not think you had the nerve to say or put so elo-
quently? Or did you make a snap decision which prevented a dis-
aster?

You might well have been receiving promptings from highly
evolved souls whose primary concern at that moment was your
and others' welfare. In which case you have probably already
been a channel and perhaps not realised it! It really is that easy
and can happen in any everyday situation. You can also use channelling for guidance about your own spiritual direction.

Of course you can put difficulties in your path if you choose
to do so by allowing your ego to say 'I can't do this' or 'I'm not
good enough,' or even 'I've been on a spiritual tack for a long
time now. Why haven't the ascended masters got in touch with
me?' The best way to approach channelling is to have an open
mind and to treat your friends in the higher realms as they do
you – with trust, respect and love.

Will I be taken over if I channel?
Trance mediums and trance channels have traditionally chosen
to let energies blend with or, as the person hinted to Louise,
overshadow them, thereby allowing higher dimensional beings
to use a physical body to speak through. This is usually a conscious decision and is dependent on the channel metaphorically

stepping back to allow someone else to take centre stage in a borrowed costume. However, now that greater numbers of people are coming into their own mastery, the ascended masters are encouraging a different sort of communication, more of a two-way, free-flowing chat which does not depend on one party temporarily relinquishing any part of themselves or their power.

How will I know if I'm connecting with an ascended master?
The most obvious feature is likely to be the feeling of unconditional love which may surge through your body or focus on your heart centre. It may be so overwhelming that it unleashes floods of tears, but levels of intensity will vary according to your state of wellbeing, your receptivity and/or the appropriateness of the occasion.

If you are not overcome by strong sensations, don't worry! Your ascended friend(s) may be of the opinion that you will respond better to other signs, such as a gentle warmth or tingling in a particular part of your body.

Be open to any possibility, and if you are not sure ask for the signal to be strengthened so that you can always recognise it from the background norm. In time you will work out a code between you which works well for both/all of you – remember that it might not only be you who is new to this game. Patience, understanding and practice will reap dividends in the long run.

As I mentioned in Chapter 2 (see page 23), don't get too hung up on names or be disappointed if one of the top guns does not come through for you. If you would really like to link with a chohan or one of the world teachers, then ask – be specific and know that your request will have been heard. You are perfectly entitled to communicate with any ascended master.

Since like attracts like, it is doubtful you will ever encounter any unruly low vibrational energy which is obstructive, unhelpful or misleading. Nevertheless discernment should always be exercised – in fact it will be expected of you. So never pussyfoot around if you are not sure of the contact you are making or if you are uneasy about any aspect of a channelling session.

Trust your instincts and ask three times for confirmation that you are linking with the highest dimensional being suitable for your current level of spiritual evolution. By spiritual law you must receive a truthful answer.

If you are still unsure, ask for the energy to depart and then invoke the violet flame for yourself. It's not a case of being fearful, merely the chance for you to assert your mastery and demand the best possible learning opportunity for yourself. None of the ascended masters will take offence if you ask them to leave because it does not feel right for you.

Is there a protocol for channelling?
There is no prescribed wording or method you have to follow, because intent and willingness to try are probably the most important prerequisites. As you gain confidence as a master you may find it more meaningful to devise your own way of doing things, but if you prefer a few guidelines to get you started you might break the process down into five elements:

• protection (see page 63)
• invoke the violet flame (see page 65)
• request to connect with the ascended realms (ask for the highest level being(s) appropriate for your spiritual growth/highest good – you deserve it!) and ask for guidance/spiritual knowledge/questions, etc for yourself and/or others
• link with an ascended master (or masters if, for example, you are seeking guidance on a number of issues) and receive communication; if appropriate, work out questions beforehand – in time you may wish to enter a dialogue and be able to improvise as you go along
• offer thanks for the occasion however well or otherwise you think it has gone, and make a note of events.

Can mediums channel ascended masters?
The quick answer to that is a resounding yes, if they so wish. Mediums dedicate themselves to providing people with evidence of life after death, essentially by passing on apparently mundane though usually very poignant messages from loved ones in the fourth dimension. But as part of their own development they

may feel the need to expand their horizons. Many do in fact find themselves naturally wanting to offer clients guidance based on greater spiritual knowledge. And this is where channelling the ascended realms can obviously be of huge benefit all round.

Liz, a medium brimming with vitality and enthusiasm, was interested in bringing the violet flame into her work, so Louise and I visited her with the intention of trying out some of the new invocations. After chatting for a while we turned our attention to Liz's mediumship and speculated about the difference it might make to her if all three of us recited words together before she gave a reading. Although Liz was quite familiar with the seventh ray as a healing energy, she had never specifically called upon it as a prelude to her clairvoyance.

We decided there and then to go ahead with our trio invocation, assuming there would be some sort of enhancement. We were not wrong! As soon as we had finished, Liz's characteristic chirpiness deserted her. She was stunned into unusual silence while Louise and I looked at one another, astonished at her reaction. It took her a while to compose herself, but when she did she explained what has turned out to be a literally life-changing experience for her.

Apparently she was taken completely unawares by an extremely forceful energy that made its presence felt straight after the invocation. It was unfamiliar to her and so strong that she was not immediately sure how to deal with it.

As she enjoys a closeness with the angelic kingdom, she asked Archangel Raphael and Archangel Michael to step the energy down for her so that she could cope with it more easily. Her request was heard and a slide, the sort found in children's playgrounds, appeared to her in gold. She was given the impression that this symbol represented a new link for her with the higher dimensions.

Since then she has learned that the powerful being who arrived unannounced was none other than ascended master El Morya, chohan of the blue ray. She has now adjusted to his vibration and those of many other cosmic friends who regularly provide her with information via her golden slide. Liz practically purrs with contentment: she says her awareness of the angelic realms has significantly increased many fold, and she has never before felt so peaceful and full of love.

What are the different ways of channelling?
There are any number of ways to channel, but the key to most is to raise your own vibration as much as you can beforehand, to clear your mind and to concentrate from within your heart centre.

You can do the first by saying positive affirmations out loud, invoking the violet flame, listening to uplifting music, thinking loving thoughts, lighting a candle, having a relaxing bath or shower, reading an inspirational book, doing breathing exercises – anything which allows you to calm and centre yourself.

You no doubt have favourite ways of uncluttering your mind, but try a few new ones from time to time. Their novelty may prevent your brain taking advantage of the familiar and allowing inner chatter to talk over the top of what you are seeking to achieve. If you have ever grown so accustomed to an affirmation that while you're saying it you find yourself thinking about what you are going to have to eat in the next few minutes, you will know what I mean.

With practice you will be able to attain a receptive state within minutes or even seconds, and eventually it will become a natural part of your make-up. Once you have prepared yourself and called upon the ascended masters, have confidence in yourself and your abilities. Allow whatever is to happen to unfold effortlessly for you – you should never need to force the issue.

It may take several sessions before in your terms you make progress, because adjustments to your spiritual (and physical) receptors may have to take place first. You may notice odd noises or sensations in your head and neck especially. Don't be put off if this happens: it is a good sign and means wheels are being set in motion for you.

Many people start off by attempting verbal channelling. In a nutshell this means expressing out loud what you sense through feelings, thoughts, images or actual words heard as your inner voice or as someone else's spoken voice. To begin with it can be a little like putting yourself in the spotlight and not knowing your lines. You might feel as though you are making things up, and then be self-conscious about articulating them. This does not matter at all, for by allowing yourself to let go and speak you are learning to pay close attention to your senses and body and are becoming attuned to higher vibrations.

The ascended masters will be doing all they can to put you at your ease, but they are not you in your physical vessel so always let them know if you feel overly uncomfortable. Their admiration and love for you are so vast that your every action will be blessed.

If verbal channelling does not suit or appeal to you, you might like to consider alternatives. Think about your favourite pastimes or what you are good at – do they present you with opportunities to channel? You may wish to keep special third dimensional hobbies out of the spiritual equation, and that is always a good, healthy attitude to adopt.

If, however, you are willing to experiment, you may find it easier to relax into channelling when you are doing something which already comes naturally to you. You may also be able to distinguish more easily between usual activity and that which is new territory. Here are a few suggestions to set the ball rolling.

Writing

As well as asking questions in your head, you can write them down on a piece of paper or type them out on a computer. This helps you clarify what it is you are requesting. Then simply allow your pen or fingers to form whatever words and phrases come to you without you thinking about or prejudging the responses.

A healer once recommended that you formulate the questions with your dominant writing hand, and use your other hand to take down the answers. This temporarily cuts off the logical, analytical side of your brain and frees up your spiritual channels. It is also harder for your ego to assert itself – always beware of your ego's potential to influence you, especially when you are learning the ropes. Check in with your heart centre to establish whether what you receive vibrates with love.

After a particularly vivid dream of mine in which the main character told me I had committed suicide in World War I, I wondered whether using this technique would give me an insight into what naturally came as quite a shock – although as a young child I distinctly remember going for a walk in some woods with my father and carrying a pretend gun while moving from bush to bush in evasive army-type manoeuvres (this was untypical behaviour for me and happened just the once).

I had not really attempted channelling before, but I worked out that if I scribbled impressions as they came to me and did not try to finish off sentences as I thought they should be, I ended up with some very interesting comments.

There was a fine line between words selected by my conscious mind and those apparently entering my head of their own accord. I was particularly intrigued by the response to 'Is there much karma from this suicide incident that is currently affecting me?' What unravelled on the page through my spidery lettering was, 'There is a confusion between your expectations and your belief patterns.' Quite a philosophical gem.

Composition

If you like writing fiction, prose or poetry, call upon the ascended realms for a master who can inspire you and help bring out the very best in you. Jot down whatever springs out of the ether or ask for help whenever you dry up.

A friend put the theory into practice and keyed in on the computer what turned out to be the bare bones for a poem. A string of words, which at first seemed random and unrelated, led to a curious scenario he could see vividly and feel in his mind's eye. From there it was a matter of fleshing out the details. The creative process was very different from what he was accustomed to and was most enjoyable as well as productive.

While writing this book I always asked for guidance each day. Sometimes words would tumble through my fingers at great speed, as though my thought processes had been accelerated, and these were often accompanied by surges of energy which flowed through my body and simultaneously manifested as sparkling crackles on the computer screen. In a couple of instances the text area even shrank substantially inwards briefly too before returning to normal.

It is interesting to note that the greatest help was extended when I was trying to explain the most 'difficult' concepts and was searching for precise wording. On these occasions it felt as though someone was standing behind me, leaning over my right shoulder. For the rest of the time there were many flashes of blue around the computer and particularly the keyboard, but I sensed I was basically being left to deal with style and content on my own. However, neither Louise nor I would have had our involvement in this project any other way. If the whole book had been dictated to us line by line it would have been very boring for us – not our style at all. And, most importantly, we would have learned little about being masters.

If you're a musician, however good, bad or indifferent, close your eyes, put your hands into a ready position, and open yourself up to new possibilities. Don't shy away from odd sounds – listen out for tunes in amongst them and have a go at reproducing them. Or just allow your fingers to move wherever they want to. If you're not too embarrassed, set a tape recorder running and then try to forget about it while you concentrate on playing from your heart.

Artists, too, can learn to go with the flow. Even if you have never picked up a paintbrush in your life, you might be amazed by what you can do. Patrick, a builder by trade whose aptitude for painting used to go no further than decorating walls and skirting boards, now produces the most astonishing pictures in oils of angels and guides. When working with spiritual helpers his work is tremendously skilful and deeply moving, and it has transformed his life as well as taught others many universal truths.

And yet without assistance from the higher dimensions, he cannot do more than draw a few squiggles.

Angel/divining cards

Simply use these in the normal way, and invite the ascended realms to convey messages through them. If you don't have a suitable set, you could devise your own with pictures, words and phrases that are pertinent to you and perhaps your current situation. Think laterally when making your list of subjects.

Whenever you select a card and its meaning is not immediately apparent, pause and wait for a message. In fact it's probably a good habit to adopt anyway, because the first and obvious interpretation may not be what is actually intended.

In time you may be able to dispense with the cards, for you will know what is being said to you before you've even picked them up. It's really like having a prop and then building enough confidence to throw it away and manage without it.

Meditation and dreams

Meditation is the choice of many people, since they find the relaxed state of openness increases their receptivity – although you do not have to enter a deep meditation to make a connection with an ascended master. Group settings in which members are supportive of one another and of a common objective can also raise vibrations and greatly help the process along, although it has to be said that not every one is comfortable channelling in these conditions. If you prefer to be on your own, follow that instinct.

Keep a notepad or tape recorder near you so that you can record your experiences afterwards. As you become more proficient you may be able to do this during your sessions without breaking your concentration.

Dreams, too, are an excellent means by which we are given hints and direction because, unlike the waking state, there is no pressure on us to perform. Make your requests before you are too sleepy – write them down if you're likely to have forgotten them by the morning – and then allow yourself to drift off, safe in the knowledge that all will be dealt with by the next day.

Is it up to me to make the first move?
There is no definitive answer to this question, as it really depends on what you believe and what you and your soul wish to happen. As you are likely to have been contacted already by an array of ascended masters, it may be more a case of how much you want to bring the communication onto a conscious level.

However, sometimes ascended masters will make their unsolicited presence markedly known to certain individuals they intend to work with very closely. This can be disconcerting when it comes unexpectedly, but invariably after a period of adjustment the relationship is cherished by both parties.

The ultimate in channelling

Marian is a pragmatic, down to earth person who works with senior executives in large businesses, encouraging them to fulfil their potential by creating nurturing, stimulating environments for themselves and their staff. She needs to be able to assess people and situations very quickly, and does this by picking up on their energies – sometimes seeing them as round or angular shapes – and putting them through her own personal filter of past observations and experiences.

While Marian is following a spiritual path, channelling ascended beings from other dimensions is a real turn off for her; she prefers to find solutions to problems 'from within' herself. She agrees she has a highly developed intuition but has still been slightly perplexed by recent developments which enable her to tell people facts about themselves she herself is not aware of. Even though she does not formulate them in her mind beforehand, these can be extremely accurate; as she says, 'they just come through' from, she presumes, her inner wisdom.

Here are a couple of incidents to explore further this idea of regularly accessing your own resources, a theme which, as I mentioned at the start of the chapter, will become increasingly important for all masters.

The first occurred when Louise had a few minutes to spare while running a bath. She tried a quick mirror experiment and invoked the violet flame. After brilliant golden light appeared round her head, Saint Germain's face was then superimposed over her own, and after that followed in rapid succession each of the seven chohans plus Sananda, Kuthumi and other well-known ascended masters.

This sequence was repeated, but before it could happen a third time Louise's attention was diverted to the bath which by now was almost overflowing! She could not wait for the mirror scenes to reach their natural conclusion, but wondered whether the faces of the ascended masters represented the divine qualities she had now fully accessed, like Marian, to enable her to be a master too in her own right.

A few months later Louise and I arranged to attend a large mind, body and spirit fair to meet Angela who specialises in aura photography. We intended to have a series of photographs taken after we had each separately made different affirmations/decrees, hoping they would provide visual evidence of the effects of these on energies around us. Angela kindly agreed to assist us and duly took a number of shots (see the pictures on pages 166 and 167).

We waited expectantly for the polaroids to develop, but as the colours began to appear we looked at one another with puzzled expressions. They were not what we had imagined, although by now we should have known better than to anticipate a particular outcome!

Angela's quick overall interpretation at the time had been that the photographs showed a general building up of Christ energy and the energy of masters. Louise and I met up a few weeks later and scrutinised them again very hard, believing they had yet further information to divulge. By the end of a long morning batting ideas backwards and forwards we came to appreciate fully what had been revealed to us through our aura pictures.

The first of the sequences, the scientific controls, are uncannily similar and highlight a balance between physical practicality and spirituality. The second of Louise's pictures shows the powerful effect of the violet flame invocation, while mine shows how the simple affirmation 'I AM a Master' even without the violet flame can soon begin clearing and refining energy. The third shots are the most intriguing. In Louise's, bright colours arch over the top of her golden aura, while in mine the lower third of the photograph is divided equally between pink on my left and blue on my right, and the upper two thirds are predominantly gold.

We kept being drawn again and again to these photographs, but did not understand why. As we had been discussing various aspects of ascension, Louise fetched a picture both of us probably glance at most days. It was the 'Chart of your Divine Self' and she felt it might trigger something for us. This striking painting is featured in several of Elizabeth Clare Prophet's books and is a figurative representation of the different stages of ascension – the physical body merging first with the Christ consciousness and then with the I AM presence or soul.

Louise and I have always understood the painting and most particularly its colours to have been channelled from the ascended realms and so we kept casting our eyes backwards and forwards, searching for vital clues.

Then came what we describe as another eureka moment. We stared at the divine self painting: the lower physical body is enveloped in pink and the middle Christ consciousness in blue, while the I AM presence is a series of coloured concentric rings, the large inner circular core of which is gold and light.

Their colours – also, significantly, the same as the three-fold flame, symbol of the divine spark – matched those in my third photograph. (The wonderful artwork we feel privileged to be able to reproduce on pages 164 and 165 is another artist's beautiful, more recent interpretation of these aspects of ourselves. The I AM presence in Graham's representation, which also appears on the cover of this book, largely reflects the colours of unconditional love.)

I thought back to the decree I used before it was taken and to the precise wording. I did not specify a master by name, nor did I invite a master into my aura, but I did call on anyone who had been working on the book (Louise's wording was very similar.)

Although Louise and I had felt the familiar energy of the ascended masters while we had been waiting for Angela at the fair, they must have been keeping a respectful distance and, as requested, did not enter our auras. So perhaps the master being shown in my third picture was the one in the third dimension who had been beavering away writing each day for the past six months – in other words me! And the positioning of the colours suggested that merging with the Christ consciousness had recently taken place and that the higher self was drawing near.

With that astonishing thought in mind we soon grasped that we should now make calling on our higher selves a priority. Shortly afterwards Louise seized the opportunity of an evening of group channelling exercises led by Ashian to practise and was shocked by what happened.

She determined at the outset that she would ask her higher self, rather than an ascended master, to make its presence felt. While she was settling into her chair, a beautiful vibrant violet energy sparkling with Source light moved quickly across a wall to her right.

Then, as time went by, she detected an energy shift around her and felt an odd feeling in her chest. In the past she had always associated this sensation with Saint Germain but because she was now focusing on her I AM presence she assumed it was that. She asked for the connection to be strengthened and the tightness in her chest increased, so much so she vaguely wondered whether she was near to suffering a heart attack.

Members of the group then concentrated on inviting an ascended master into the centre of their circle; Louise knew instinctively it would be Saint Germain and she was soon proved right. She continued sensing the strong presence behind her, and while other people were speaking round about her she could only sit quietly as what felt like invisible psychic surgery was performed on her heart centre.

At this point Ashian gave a list of Saint Germain's past incarnations to someone to read out aloud. As soon as she heard the first few lines Louise was moved to tears and fervently hoped she would not be asked to read anything, for she knew her emotional response would be too much for her to contain. Throughout this experience she was confused about why, when she was supposedly linking with her higher self, she was feeling such a strong connection with the chohan of the seventh ray.

After she went home and was talking it all through with Andy, the mist of bewilderment lifted: she remembered in the dim and distant past reading about the higher self being the means by which the ascended masters send us messages and we likewise can contact them. In other words the higher self can be interpreted as another way of describing our light body or golden communication grid – it's like being hooked in to a giant cosmic internet, and having access to everyone in the universe...

A more appropriate term for the manner in which the ascended masters communicate with us via our I AM presence is 'overlighting' – they allow us to stand firm in our own radiance, while their light and inspiration embrace rather than invade our space. The closer your higher self is to you, the nearer the point of communication and the stronger your sense of the ascended masters' presence will be – as experienced by Louise to make the point crystal clear to her during the channelling evening, and beautifully illustrated in the third of her photographs in which coloured energies of the ascended masters are above, not within, her golden aura.

Over to you

Do you understand now why channelling your higher self is one of the most meaningful and satisfying things you can do?

By linking first with your I AM presence or your light body, you connect with the very purest aspect of yourself – God in you – and, as like attracts like (and light attracts light) you draw to you only the very best for yourself. On that basis it makes spiritual sense to connect with your divine I AM presence as much as you can. By so doing you can also tap into your own divine wisdom, your fund of intimate knowledge about yourself and the cosmos (see again Paul's picture on page 168). You really can be self-sufficient, a master of the universe – everything can be accessed from within your own energy field.

And on that uplifting note, I come to the end of our book. It is now up to you how and when you use your wonderful ascension gifts. Believe in yourself and through your miracles make your path as easy for yourself as you can. You deserve no less than the very best – always.

Until we have the pleasure of meeting again, I leave you with three inspirational lines from John Milton's appropriately titled poem *Paradise Regained*. Although written well over three hundred years ago, they sum up practically all that can be said today about being a master:

> *...he who receives*
> *Light from above, from the fountain of light,*
> *No other doctrine needs...*

CHAPTER 9

Affirmations, decrees and invocations

Here are some extra affirmations you can use or adapt to help you in your life as a master of the universe. Remember that by getting into the habit of calling upon your higher self you will create the very best for yourself.

Say each three times and follow with 'Let it be so. So it is.' to seal your commitment.

To start the day

I AM a Master. I now call to me the love, light, energy and presence of my Higher Self.

Daily affirmation of your mastery

I AM a Master.

I AM a Divine Being of Light living in a physical body.

I AM pure of Heart, offering love and compassion to all.

I AM pure of Mind, seeing everything in a
non-judgemental way.

I AM pure of Soul, knowing that life unfolds perfectly
and for the highest good of all.

I AM willing to be of service in whatever way
is appropriate.

I AM able to honour the Divine within every aspect
of creation.

I AM ready and willing to communicate with other
Beings of Light in the Ascended Realms.

I AM here to teach by example.

I AM forgiveness.

I AM Light.

I AM Love.

I AM a Master of Light.

As a prelude to personal affirmations and requests

> I AM a Master and I call to me the Light of my Higher
> Self. Through my I AM Presence I am creating for myself
> now...

For protection and as a general spring clean

> I AM a Master and I call to me the Light of my Higher
> Self. Through my I AM Presence I invoke the Violet
> Flame to transmute energy in and around me and trans-
> form it into Light.

Using the symbol of protection

While saying '*I AM a Master and I now seal myself with the sign
of protection*' visualise light coming out from your heart centre,
moving up over your head, down your back and legs, under your
feet and up the front of your body to your heart.

Pause for a few seconds.

Then visualise light again emanating from your heart centre
and this time moving along the front of your right arm, round
your hand, along the back of your arm, across your back, along
your left arm, round your left hand, along the front of your arm
and once more back to your heart centre.

The cross of light you have made symbolises unity of matter
and spirit, and affords powerful protection.

For protection of others

> I AM a Master and I call to me the Light of my Higher
> Self. Through my I AM Presence I now seal [insert
> name(s) of people/vehicles/situations, etc] with the
> protection of Divine Light.

For healing

> I AM a Master and I call to me the Light of my Higher
> Self. Through my I AM Presence I now invoke healing
> energies for [insert name of people, place, etc].

For beginning meditation or before going to sleep
(or even if you're sitting down quietly for 5 minutes rest)

> I AM a Master and I call to me the Light of my Higher
> Self. Through my I AM Presence I am now asking my
> Higher Self to communicate wisdom, knowledge or
> insights that are in line with my highest good.

If you don't feel as though you are a master, use this to boost your confidence:

> I AM a Master and I call to me the energies and qualities
> of the ascended realms. I am now ready to integrate these
> qualities into my life.

For channelling

> I AM a Master and I call to me the Light of my Higher
> Self. Through my I AM Presence I am now ready to
> communicate with the Masters of the Ascended Realms.
> I call forth Ascended Master [name] and I give
> permission for his/her energy to connect with mine in
> order that we may communicate easily.

A quick version of the violet flame invocation to help others

> I AM a Master and I invoke the Violet Flame to cleanse
> this person/place/situation now.

Master guidelines

As a final summary, here are some guidelines to being a Master of Light. The statements may seem obvious, but you may find it's helpful to remind yourself of them from time to time:

Believe you are worthy
Nothing can ever take away from you your divinity. And being divine means accepting yourself for who and what you are – an important cog in the celestial wheel: without your contribution, it would grind to a halt. Similarly:

Honour the divine in all people, creatures and other
manifestations within your world

Loving intent is everything
From intent springs manifestation: you are a co-creator from the heart with The Source and can bring heaven to earth.

Know and love yourself
Use whatever tools and techniques you feel are appropriate for you to help you work through your issues. Learn when to be gentle with yourself and when to push yourself hard.

Always forgive yourself and others
Everyone, including yourself, is doing the best they can with the knowledge they have at any given moment. So do not judge – you may not have the whole picture.

Be mindful of your thoughts, as they create your reality.
When asking for something, be as specific as you can: the universe has a habit of taking requests literally. Check wayward thoughts or spoken words by saying simply 'I cancel that!'

Know and trust that all events and situations unfold in perfect timing according to the divine plan.

How many times have you looked back and realised everything worked out for the best? Probably dozens.

So when you next catch yourself becoming frustrated by lack of progress in particular areas of your life, remember you will be looking back in a few months and laughing.

Similarly, embrace change, for it inevitably brings new opportunities for growth. Resisting it may set up barriers to health and harmony.

Love unconditionally and be of service to others without expecting thanks in physical terms.

Your actions will always be acknowledged on a spiritual level.

View life from a higher spiritual perspective

Step back from people and situations and ask yourself, 'How would a master react or behave in this scenario?' And in time you will be able to cut this down to: 'Don't think! Just BE a Master of Light!'

Meditation: 'To be a Master of Light'

In this meditation you will connect and merge with your higher self. The more often you do this, the more in tune you will become with your soul and the part you are playing in the divine plan.

Take yourself to a quiet place where you won't be disturbed and ideally wear loose, comfortable clothing. Sit with your feet firmly on the floor and have your hands on your knees or thighs, or in your lap. Close your eyes.

Take a deep breath, hold it for a moment and then breathe out, affirming to yourself 'I AM a Master'. Take another deep breath, hold it and breathe out, once again affirming to yourself 'I AM a Master'. Do this a third time and really believe it when you say 'I AM a Master'.

Be aware of feelings or sensations in your body. Don't waste your energy by worrying about them, but instead affirm to yourself, 'I AM a Divine Being of Light living in a physical body, I AM a Divine Being of Light living in a physical body, I AM a Divine Being of Light living in a physical body'.

As a master, you are now going to use the powerful energy of the violet flame. You have been given this tool to help you on your ascension path. It is a tool of spiritual alchemy which symbolically can turn base metal into gold.

During your many incarnations you have changed, and you have become that base metal. But your true form is golden. Within you is the very essence of the Creator, your divine spark or threefold flame containing the Will, Wisdom and Love of God. It is time to reconnect to the real you by invoking the violet flame.

Move your awareness to your heart centre. You may like to visualise the blue, yellow and pink of the threefold flame while you say to yourself, 'I AM a Master. I invoke the violet flame to transmute the energy in and around me, and transform it into Light'. Immediately the violet flame begins to work on you, its energy easing sensations in your body.

Say a second time, 'I AM a Master. I invoke the violet flame to transmute the energy in and around me, and transform it into Light'. You may be aware of warmth and a feeling of relaxation. Your cares and worries drift away. Affirm for a third time, 'I AM a Master. I invoke the violet flame to transmute the energy in and around me, and transform it into Light'.

Now you really begin to feel the power of the violet flame. Its energy is gathering around you until it becomes a swirling violet cloud. It is working on all levels of your being – your body, your emotions, your mind and your spirit. You are more at ease as you promise yourself you will now, or in the next few days, let go of all pain, fears, worries, and issues from this life or past lives that may be holding you back from transformation.

You may start to feel lighter, as though you are losing your physical form. Every cell in your body is becoming highly charged and activated. Soon you no longer identify with your physical self but see yourself as a bright geometric triangle with the upward point in place of your head. This triangle is filled with the Light and coloured energy of your true self. You may see or know what this colour is. It is probably one you have been drawn to recently, if not throughout your life. It may even be your favourite colour, but don't be concerned if you are unsure. Know it is there even if you cannot see it.

You now become aware of another triangle above you, pointing down towards you. It is also full of Light and its colour is purple tinged with magenta. Its Light increases as it hovers above you, and then it moves down and merges with your triangle so that the two form a Star of David. The combination of Light and energy is incredibly powerful and the star begins to rotate. You are caught up in the movement, and may feel a surge of extra energy.

You are pulled and lifted into a higher level of consciousness. Here there are different colours – it is like being in a sea of blues and aquamarines. Spend time absorbing the colour and vibration of the sea's waves. Be aware of their impact on your heart centre which will open and expand. Divine qualities now filter through you, qualities of compassion, forgiveness, respect, honour and love. But this is not the love we experience in our earthly relationships – it is perfect, unconditional love. Soak up its beauty and spend a few moments in its blissful peace.

Now feel your consciousness expanding yet further. It is as though there is no difference between the energy within you and the energy around you. You sense a oneness with the universe and a deeper understanding of love. You are beginning to merge with an even more intense divine Light which is sparkling with vibrant colours – violet, purple, pink, magenta, green, blue and gold. You can now, if you wish, access the spiritual knowledge that is contained within this Light. This knowledge may appear as a mass of geometric shapes. Or you may be able to communicate with other Beings of Light.

It is now time for you to blend totally with the Light and energy of your Higher Self. You notice that not only are colours all around you but they are within you too. They are moving and dancing, flowing and rippling. Suddenly you hear the sound of a roaring wind, and then the complete uniting of energies takes place. You have merged with the Light. You have become a Master of Light. Spend as long as you wish enjoying this very special connection. Know that you can return to it whenever you would like to, and reaffirm to yourself, 'I AM a Master of Light, I AM a Master of Light, I AM a Master of Light'.

You now have the ability to bring the energy of your higher self into every aspect of your life. It may even be part of your spiritual contract to do so. You may like to state your intent that from now on you will always be a Master of Light. Visualise your body and aura radiant with Light and then trace that Light back to your heart centre. Move your awareness into it and become aware of your slow and steady breathing. Then take your awareness to your hands and your feet. Move them gently and, when you are ready, open your eyes. Be present in your surroundings, understanding that as a Master of Light you can now always balance physical and spiritual matters. It is very easy for you to do.

Further reading

Access the power of your higher self, Elizabeth Clare Prophet (Summit University Press, 1997)

The Awakener: The time is now, Sandy Stevenson (Gateway, 1997)

Crystal power, crystal healing, Michael Gienger (Blandford, 1998)

Journey of souls: case studies of life between lives, Michael Newton (Llewellyn Publications, 2001)

The light shall set you free, Dr Norma Milanovich and Dr Shirley McCune (Athena Publishing, 1996)

A little light on ascension, Diana Cooper (Findhorn Press, 1997)

Lost secrets of the sacred ark, Laurence Gardner (Element, 2003)

Messages from the masters: Tapping into the power of love, Dr Brian Weiss (Piatkus, 2000)

Opening to channel: How to connect with your guide, Sanaya Roman and Duane Packer (HJ Kramer Inc, 1987)

Signposts: The universe is whispering to you, Denise Linn (Rider, 1996)

About the authors

Louise Hopkinson, teacher of drama and English for 27 years, now runs spiritual awareness workshops and courses, covering such subjects as the aura and chakras, the journey of the soul, twin flames, personal growth, the violet flame, the ascended masters and mastering ascension. If you would like details of forthcoming courses and workshops run by Louise, or if you would like to organise an event in your area with her, check out her website:

www.geocities.com/mandalagroup

Jane White began her career in bookselling and then moved into publishing from where she joined the publicity section of a government department in Whitehall. In 1997 she and her husband moved to Cornwall where they run their own local publishing business. Her first book, *Spiritual Guides in the West Country* (Bossiney Books), was published in 2001.

Louise and Jane have been exploring their spirituality for a number of years. Their interest in different forms of healing and their ability to perceive spiritual energy, often as vibrant colours, brought them together to share insights and channelled knowledge with others.

Further information

If you are interested in seeing more of Graham Cheater's digital artwork, have a look at his website:

www.theart2heal.com

For more insights and information from Sandy Stevenson, her website is: www.lightascension.com

Index